BAKING PIES
&
MAKING LOVE

The Good. The Bad. The Different.
Of Building Strong Marriages and Relationships.

BAKING PIES
&
MAKING LOVE

The Good. The Bad. The Different.
Of Building Strong Marriages and Relationships.

C. NATHANIEL BROWN

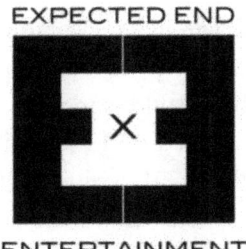

Atlanta, GA

Copyright © 2019 C. Nathaniel Brown
All rights reserved. No part of this book may be reproduced or transmitted in any form or by any means, electronic or mechanical, including photocopy, recording, or by any information storage and retrieval system with the exception of a reviewer who may quote brief passages in a review to be printed in a blog, newspaper or magazine without written permission from the author. Address inquiries to:
Expected End Entertainment,
P.O. Box 1751, Mableton, GA 30126.
Published by Expected End Entertainment/EX3 Books
ExpectedEndEntertainment@gmail.com * www.EX3ent.com
ISBN-10: 0-9968932-4-5
ISBN-13: 978-0-9968932-4-4
Printed in the United States of America

PRAISE FOR THE BOOK...

"This book is filled with such valuable information and a level of honesty that anyone in a relationship or marriage can identify with and appreciate. Being married 15 years we have been through similar things and situations and we discovered that 'growing together' is a huge part of having a successful marriage. Great book!"

- **Tristan and Nina King**

"Baking Pies and Making Love expounds on the realities of the hard work required in a marriage. If your journey has not yet begun, you will find fool proof wisdom within the pages of this book. If your journey is in progress, here is a read that I believe, will shed some light in your darkness. This book speaks to the most important ingredients in marriage...loyalty and love.

- **Arlene McGuire**

"As newlyweds, Baking Pies & Making Love is a valuable resource to help us avoid pitfalls and continue to build on a solid foundation. We recommend this book to everyone, not just newlyweds."

- **Ben and Antoinette Coleman**

MORE PRAISE FOR THE BOOK...

"Writing about two difficult concepts such as baking and love is bold but to simplify the steps and merging them into one is brilliant! The book challenges couples to maintain identify while building life together. Well done!"

— **Necole and Felix Turner**

"This book is everything a couple needs to strengthen, heal or maintain a great friendship with their spouse-while building on love and what it means to be in love. Great read!"

- **Phillip and Kenya Hendricks**

"Baking Pies and Making Love is a great resource for couples considering marriage to those in various phases of their marriage. This book emphasizes the importance of the couple finding the balance in maintaining their identity as individuals as well as continuing to grow as a couple. A much read for all couples!"

- **William and Sharise Nance**

DEDICATION

To married couples everywhere who still believe in the power of love. And to soon-to-be couples who need to know they can make it.

CONTENTS

FOREWORD .... Tarai Alexander
ACKNOWLEDGEMENTS i
INTRODUCTION iii
MAINTAIN YOUR IDENTITY 1
HOME SWEET HOME 11
LESSONS LEARNED FROM SALSA DANCING 25
MAKING LOVE 39
EXAMPLES OF LOVE 47
FAMILY AND FRIENDS 55
CHILDREARING 63
COUNSELING 77
DEALING WITH DIFFICULT TIMES 91
A PERFECT MOMENT 101
ABOUT THE AUTHOR 107

FOREWORD

Baking Pies & Making Love. It's an odd though intriguing title. A metaphor for many romantic relationships. Some days are sweet and smooth sailing. Some days strip you naked as the day you were born. Some days start in the kitchen for a bite then you end up intertwined elsewhere. Those are great days!

Baking pies usually requires a recipe. Those who have never done it before typically follow instructions to the letter, while people who are creative and know their way around sugar and spice will develop their own variations to make it even more pleasing. They use all their senses and feel it with their heart. Making love is no different. You've got your basic "put *this* in *there* and move with rhythm" but there are people who get creative, use all their senses and make the encounter better than the standard exercise. You'll need to burn the calories from the pie anyway.

With any good pie there is a blend of sweet, savory and salty ingredients. The same is true of unions. While the standard recipe for a healthy and lasting partnership starts with two bundles of love, a measure of grace and scoops of fine communication, what gets added next depends on your palate and needs. In these pages, you'll get a dash of laughs, a sprinkle of hope, a smidge of candor and several drops of reality to help enhance your mix. One thing to keep in mind when baking pies and making love is that over time your tastes may change. It's okay to adjust, not abandon, the recipe as your preferences evolve.

You can bake a pie alone but when someone you're connected to is there to help you measure, roll, beat and fill, it gets done in half the time, memories are made, and the flavor seems richer. You can't make love by yourself; some would beg to differ, but this isn't that kind of book. It takes two willing participants to open themselves up and become one breath, one heartbeat, one flesh.

Happy baking and passionate love making!

Tarai Alexander

ACKNOWLEDGEMENTS

I want to thank God for his leading and guiding and never leaving me alone. Thank you to my children and my grandchildren for fueling me to do what I do and become who I am becoming. Thank you to Team EX3 for just being you. Thank you to everyone who has been an example of greatness for me to emulate. And finally to my wife, Tarai, without you, this book would not exist.

INTRODUCTION

On August 12, 1995, as we stood at the altar of Northside Institutional Church in Pittsburgh looking into each other's eyes with smiles on our faces, we heard Pastor Roger Thomas comparing marriage to mixing the ingredients of a cake. We could see in each other's eyes that we were thrown off and wasn't sure where he was going with the analogy. But what he said made a lot of sense. He said that you have God, you add a man, you add a woman, and blend those things together. The love of God mixes in with the husband. The love of God mixes in with the wife. Together they mix their love from God and their love for God with the love they have for each other and it produces a beautiful product. All of these singularly powerful elements combine to make a phenomenally beautiful, single masterpiece.

I've cleaned up the story a bit. I've taken out the references to the eggs, butter and other ingredients used in the story to drive the point home that when you bring the right ingredients, in the right doses, and blend them together, you can make something special.

In titling this book, Baking Pies & Making Love, I wanted the play on words but I also wanted the impact that the two concepts have on building and maintaining successful marriages, relationships, families and love. Just as Pastor Thomas said on that sweltering Saturday among our closest family members and friends, our lives and our marriage have been an example to many people ever since. Some have used our mistakes as an example of what not to do and others have used our successes of what to do. In this book, I will share some things we've learned along the way through personal trials, tribulations, and triumphs; through counseling and helping others; and through watching what takes place in the world around us and the world at large.

I don't claim to be the end all be all on all things dealing with love, relationship, marriage, and family. But I do have enough experience, education, training, and acquired wisdom to be able to share what we know with the hopes of helping someone, some marriage, or some family. Who knows… that one will share what they got with another and they will pass it along and before we know it, this book will have the impact that we pray it will.

Why? We see the statistics:

- About half of all marriages end in divorce.
- In America, there is a divorce about every 13 seconds.
- One study shows that 80 percent of divorced couples cited finances as being the primary contributor to their split.
- You are 35 percent more likely to suffer a severe illness or be frequently sick if you are unhappy in a relationship or marriage.
- 49 percent of people say they are happy with their sex life, which means 51 percent are unhappy.
- One-third of American children are raised without a father. That number skyrockets for

African American children, where 54 percent are raised by single mothers.

All of these statistics proves that we have our work cut out for us as a society. So many people have decided to throw in the towel. Society in general has accepted the 'here today and gone tomorrow' mentality without a second thought. Others look from afar, shake their heads, and move on without trying to help themselves or others. We've decided to do something, anything, in an attempt to make a difference.

As a result, I came up with the idea of writing this book, Baking Pies & Making Love. Not only is it designed to help others but it is part of a process to maintain and strengthen the love that we share. Love is an ongoing process that you must work at and work on. I will discuss many aspects of the process. I will also discuss such topics as maintaining your individual identity in your marriage while building an identity as a couple; building a solid foundation for love; dealing with and defeating difficult times; finances; making love; and so much more. I'll also share a few stories that will help you relate to what we have experienced, what we are experiencing, and some things that we plan to experience as a result of us loving each other better in the future. I hope that you enjoy reading this book and that it will help you bake better pies and make sweeter love.

C. Nathaniel Brown

C. NATHANIEL BROWN

CHAPTER 1
MAINTAIN YOUR IDENTITY

I was an 18-year-old college freshman when I met Tarai. She was 20 and had already been at Denison University when I got there. She was majoring in English and thinking of becoming a judge one day. I was a history major at the time thinking I would become a lawyer. We were in the process of learning who we were and what we wanted to do with the remainder of our lives. College is supposed to help you do that, right? Well, it certainly was a place where we did a lot of experimenting and formulating many of the identity traits that uniquely identify who we are becoming.

We often joke about who was attracted to whom first. Of course, she says I was interested in her and pursued her. And my version of the story is different, and the truth, I might add. She saw this strikingly handsome and charming freshmen they used to call fresh meat and she pursued me. We laugh about the differences in stories.

When I arrived on campus, she had a boyfriend and we did not learn more about each other until sometime later. We were simply two of the few black students on a predominantly white campus in the middle of Ohio. So sure we were familiar enough to see some things like how we interacted with people, what made us laugh, and what type of things we liked such as music, clothing, and the arts. But one thing neither of us imagined at that time was that we'd be together 30 years later and have raised a family.

There were some individual qualities in each of us that the other grew to love. That didn't mean either of us was perfect but obviously we were perfect enough for each other.

So, do opposites really attract? Yes and no. There are

some things that just work like our mixture of Tarai being an extrovert and my being an introvert are necessary at times, (although I have come out of my shell a lot more over the years). But if two people are on opposite sides of the fence on crucial matters such as whether to have children, religious beliefs, or monogamy, then it might be too many hurdles to overcome. When you know who you are, know your core morals and values, and what makes you happy, it makes it easier to enter a relationship confidently.

It is imperative in a relationship and marriage that you maintain your identify or you become someone that you don't like. That doesn't mean there is not give and take but what it means is that you maintain what makes you authentically you.

So, how do you do that?

First, you have to discover who you are and what makes you you. What are your core morals and values? What are the things that you enjoy most, by yourself and with others? What would you be doing if money wasn't an issue? What makes you smile, laugh and spit out your drink in amusement? What makes you cry? What hurts your heart every time you hear it or see it? What's most important to you? Children? Money? Sex? Love? Career? You have to find out what makes you tick, independent of anyone else including your spouse, family, friends, and even enemies.

Embrace it. Once you have clearly identified those things, embrace them. They make you unique, they make you special, and they make you you. But if you don't acknowledge them for yourself and embrace them, they are simply fantasies. We have enough fantasies in our lives. We have to learn to embrace all the things that make us who we are including our appearance, our thought process and the things that we like and dislike. It's loving yourself with all your flaws and imperfections.

Pursue it. If you like stage plays, find out about the local theatre companies in your area. Get on their mailing lists so you can be informed of their upcoming events. And go! If you enjoy acting and want to be a part of one of those companies, do it. If you are a thrill seeker and want to skydive, conquer the world's biggest rollercoasters, scuba dive, go after it.

Develop it. If you are business-minded, find out how to develop your passion into your profession. Research and figure out how to get to a certain point to show you are serious about it. If you want to write a book, get the ideas out of your head and onto paper. Do an outline. Research. Be in the mindset of building and developing the things that interest you.

Share it. Get your passion to the point where you are confident and prepared to share it with others. Show your husband that your passion for the arts goes beyond just watching a musical on television, that it helped you gain your confidence as a performer. Explain to your wife that your collection of model cars reminds you of your childhood relationship with your dad and is not just an insignificant waste of time.

Notice that I never mentioned another person until Step 4. You have invested so much into yourself by Step 4 that you realize that it doesn't matter who can or cannot appreciate you for who you are because you are now confident in yourself and the things that make you tick. Of course, you want people around you, especially your significant other, to appreciate you and support you. But that shouldn't define you or determine your happiness within yourself.

Tarai and I don't always agree on everything. We don't always enjoy the same things. Sometimes, they have caused friction in our marriage. Sometimes, we just couldn't understand why the other person thought or felt the way they did. She enjoyed going out more than I did. I enjoyed relaxing at home. What we spent money on differed. What we thought the other should wear at different functions differed. Arts versus sports. Quiet time alone versus out with family and friends. Her idea of celebrating her birthday is a big deal. She likes extravagant things. For my birthday, she'd ask me what I wanted or wanted to do and I'd say, "I want pizza and I want to chill at home with my family." Because of what she wanted for her birthday, she couldn't understand the simplicity of what I wanted for mine. But that was what was important to me… my favorite food and the people that make me tick.

Because of so many differences, I've often thought, "I will never be able to make her completely happy." And I believed that. Sometimes, I felt so defeated by not being able to meet her expectations, support her individual interests or determine the things that mattered most at those times. When we went through difficult times, I'd think back on all of the differences and wondered how we made it as far as we did. We've both thought at times that maybe we were not made for each other, which is a hard thing to think when you have invested so much into your marriage.

But we are learning, even after knowing each other for 30 years and being marriage for almost 24 years, we still desire to get to know each other, figure out what we bring to the marriage and what is important to each other in the marriage.

We've also learned that as we continually invest in our marriage, we must invest equally in ourselves as individuals, sometimes even more. It's not always about what can I do for the marriage; it's what can I do for myself that will enhance the marriage. That's discovering who you are, what you are good at, what you are uncomfortable with, and what you want out of the relationship. It's certainly an ongoing process because we change. So if we change, that also means the dynamics of the marriage change as well.

They say that opposites attract but we all know that opposites repel, too. So, we must learn how to make our differences work as we build or they will destroy. Many marriages have fallen apart because couples have identified their individuality but not in the context of the bigger picture. Remain in the process and remain committed to yourself *and* the relationship.

Yes, I have felt defeated because of the differences in Tarai and me. Yes, I have felt at times that our relationship was over. Yes, I've felt that she just didn't get me. Yes, I've felt like she took me for granted. Yes, I've felt like I was giving up who I was for the sake of the marriage. Yes, I've felt like I couldn't fully appreciate who I was because of how she felt about certain things. But guess what? She felt the same way.

We have to refocus our thinking as we develop and maintain our identities in our relationships. I remember telling my wife that I didn't want to split, then become the man that I desired to be, and share that person with someone else. When you are part of a team, you want to develop yourself so that you can complement the team. That's what I wanted. I have tried to take that hard look in the mirror and decided that I'm going to be a better me and that should benefit the people we love the most. The people we love should feel the same way.

Tarai and I have had a lot of difficult conversations in 30 years. But one of the things that I learned from her, especially during those conversations, is that she loves herself. She loves who she is and she loves who she is becoming. That is so attractive to me. I know that she is still evolving, still discovering the things she likes, the things she wants, and the things that make her uncomfortable.

I am too. And that's a good thing. I keep saying, living things grow and growing things live. It's a part of the process. I am committed to learning more about myself, embracing who I am, pursuing who I am, developing who I am, and sharing who I am. That's how I am going to be happy as I grow. That's how I'm going to fulfill my life's mission to be a positive example in word and deed to inspire, encourage and motivate others to dream bigger, live their dreams and impact their world.

If sports, fashion, acting, fitness, baking, and making

love are important to you and are a part of your identity, embrace them, pursue them, develop them and share them. Never lose who you are for the sake of someone else. But don't look at it as you have to choose; look at it as you are becoming a better person you for those you love the most.

We have to do a better job of introducing ourselves to our spouse on a regular bases so they can understand what is important to us. If we don't talk about them, they carry and act on their assumptions which can be a disaster. They might also feel that we don't care enough to share them. I know I've been guilty of that a few times. On the flipside, we have to have the same amount of passion in learning our spouses and what makes them who they are and who they are becoming. That should be just as much of a priority if they are a part of who you are.

I encourage Tarai to grow but I haven't always done a good job of sharing my growth with her or inquiring about her growth. And we haven't always done a great job of growing. Some years ago, I wrote a poem that I would've included if I knew where it was. But the essence of the poem said that we were ships in the middle of the ocean, passing in the dark of night. We were both on a journey but we weren't going together. At the time, we were both engulfed in our jobs; so busy in ministry that we were taking separate cars to and from church; taking turns transporting our son to events; and pursuing individual interests without the other. Individually, it appeared that things were going great. But as a couple, we were co-existing, drifting aimlessly wherever the currents took us.

So, we have to be intentional with maintaining our

individual identities but we also have to bring it together with our spouse. When that doesn't happen, many couples "grow" a part. But shouldn't we be growing together *and* in the same direction?

So how do we do that? We must:

1. **Continue to introduce yourself to your spouse.** Let them know who you are and who you are becoming. Let them know what makes you tick. They might not know why you do the things you do or act the way you act. It could make the difference in an argument or in comforting support. You can have a simple conversation with questions around a certain topic or you can be creative and play games.

2. **Get to know your spouse.** Just like you, your spouse is growing and evolving. You have to take the same action you have for them knowing and understanding you and make them an integral part of your personal development. Knowledge is power.

3. **Appreciate, support, and encourage each other's interests.** Maybe you can do it alone, but how much more would you enjoy the journey to have your spouse with you, supporting and encouraging you? Take the initiative and start supporting your spouse, letting him/her know how much you appreciate their gifts and talents and their desire to pursue what's in their heart.

Let them know that when one of you succeed you both succeed.

4. **Find ways to grow together.** Find a common interest and do it together as much as you can. It helps you introduce yourself to your spouse easier; you get to know them better; and you can appreciate, support and encourage them at the same time. Like dancing. I'll share the example of Tarai and I salsa dancing later. Making love is an excellent way to grow together. Tarai and I also love experimenting in the kitchen and we still plan to take cooking classes together. Joint interests and activities are other ways of accentuating the positives.

Tarai and I both use an example when coaching or counseling that I think will bring the point to an end. When you are on an airplane, the flight attendant gives instructions about what to do in cases of emergency. He or she says: "Secure your oxygen mask before assisting others." This is a powerful message that can be applied to so many areas of our lives. In this context, we must have our own identity before we can expect our marriage to have an identity. I can't expect my wife to understand me if I don't first understand myself. Take a proactive approach to learning yourself, maintaining your identity, and then working with your spouse to have a strong marriage where you both remain strong individually and even stronger as a couple. You can do it.

CHAPTER 2
HOME SWEET HOME

Home is where the heart is. But what does that really mean?

Most people agree there is a difference between a house and a home. They will say that a house is a physical structure where people live and a home is what you turn a house into after adding things that are special... people, love, morals, and values. Hence, the matters of the heart. I read one definition for home that said it's a place where people live permanently. I thought that was an interesting twist, especially for a few of the points I'd like to make in this chapter.

Some people use house and home interchangeably and in most cases that's absolutely acceptable because we understand what they mean based on the context of the conversation. So I'm going to share some context with you that I hope will help make your house a sweet home. As I share a few stories, I hope it compels you to ask yourself questions that lead you to answers that will determine how you build your home.

First, let's talk about foundation. Every house and home is uniquely built, even if contractors use the same cookie cutter blueprint they used for the other 15 houses on the cul de sac. They start by laying a solid foundation from which they can build up! We know that if the foundation is weak, the rest of the structure is vulnerable to damage and destruction.

So what is your foundation? Love? Religious beliefs? Experiences? Tradition? A combination of things? We understand that it takes multiple ingredients and a detailed process to make the cement that forms the basis for your foundation and a house. They all serve their purposes and are very important to the stability of what's being erected. Take a look at this excerpt from a cement manufacturer's website about the manufacturing process of cement:

"Cement is manufactured through a closely controlled chemical combination of calcium, silicon, aluminum, iron and other ingredients.

Common materials used to manufacture cement include limestone, shells, and chalk or marl combined with shale, clay, slate, blast furnace slag, silica sand, and iron ore. These ingredients, when heated at high temperatures form a rock-like substance that is ground into the fine powder that we commonly think of as cement.

The most common way to manufacture Portland cement is through a dry method. The first step is to quarry the principal raw materials, mainly limestone, clay, and other materials. After quarrying the rock is crushed. This involves several stages. The first crushing reduces the rock to a maximum size of about 6 inches. The rock then goes to secondary crushers or hammer mills for reduction to about 3 inches or smaller.

The crushed rock is combined with other ingredients such as iron ore or fly ash and ground, mixed, and fed to a cement kiln.

The cement kiln heats all the ingredients to about 2,700 degrees Fahrenheit in huge cylindrical steel rotary kilns lined with special firebrick. Kilns are frequently as much as 12 feet in diameter—large enough to accommodate an automobile and longer in many instances than the height of a 40-story building. The large kilns are mounted with the axis inclined slightly from the horizontal.

The finely ground raw material or the slurry is fed into the higher end. At the lower end is a roaring blast of flame, produced by precisely controlled burning of powdered coal, oil, alternative fuels, or gas under forced draft.

As the material moves through the kiln, certain elements are driven off in the form of gases. The remaining elements unite to form a new substance called clinker. Clinker comes out of the kiln as grey balls, about the size of marbles.

Clinker is discharged red-hot from the lower end of the kiln and generally is brought down to handling temperature in various types of coolers. The heated air from the coolers is returned to the kilns, a process that saves fuel and increases burning efficiency.

After the clinker is cooled, cement plants grind it and mix it with small amounts of gypsum and limestone. Cement is so fine that 1 pound of cement contains 150 billion grains. The cement is now ready for transport to ready-mix concrete companies to be used in a variety of construction projects."

What I really want you to grasp is the fact that the foundation is the most important aspect of building. This example shows you what goes into making the cement to lay that strong foundation. Look at all of the ingredients that go into making the foundation. You take some ingredients and they form one thing. You take other ingredients and they are used for a different purpose. And when they come together and lasts the process, they are now ready to build with and build upon. Notice that thru all the mixing, the heat and cold pressure, and time involved, it's used to build and not to tear down.

You need the right ingredients to begin the process of building a healthy home, a healthy marriage, a healthy family, and healthy relationships with extended family, friends, colleagues, etc. That's where your morals and values come to play. Your religious beliefs have a role in the process. Your family traditions and history are to be included. What you have learned along the way is important. What you have witnessed growing up and your experiences are thrown into the mix as well. All of these things and their individual processes form your ability or inability to produce a firm foundation on which to build.

Now, throw in all of those ingredients coming from your spouse or family members. Dealing with your ingredients alone is a major process but now you have to consider someone else's, too? Yes! When you factor in all of these areas, you understand that a solid foundation is important. But if you don't get a full understanding of what it takes to build the foundation and build it with the right ingredients and processes, you will quickly see the structural damage as you attempt to build on that weak foundation.

I started out by saying every house, every home, is different based on a lot of factors necessary for that particular house. So maybe you need more love to build it. Or more patience. Maybe you need more education or experience.

Every house, every home, every situation is different. What works in your best friend's marriage might not work in your marriage. How you raise your children might not work in your sister's house with her children. Your pastor and first lady might have a system that works perfectly for them, but it might not apply successfully to 80 percent of the congregation. Why? Because all of those ingredients that we bring into our relationships mesh differently and thereby create a different impact. Different ingredients change the process, just like our baking example. An Ivy League experience, suburban environment, a privileged lifestyle, and a family history that knows no different create a different ethos than someone's who has never gone to college, was born and raised in a gang-infested community, and has a family history of poverty. The way you think would be different. Your expectations would be different. The way you handle business would be different. So, if one couple told the other couple how to raise their children, how effective would it be?

Do what works for you and your home, not what someone else does or even what someone else thinks you should do. I'm not saying that you shouldn't consider other people's advice and opinions but use them as part of the ingredients as you form your foundation and build your home.

So love, experiences, personalities, traditions, education, environment, emotions, and much more go into developing your foundation. Let's look at a few areas within a home and relationships that we have to consider and work on constantly as we build. We can think of these areas as pillars or support beams in our construction.

Love

Not only is love a major part of the foundation, it is one of the most important aspects in building the rest of the house. It is a pillar and support beam. It is, as the song says, what the world needs more of. Certainly, our homes need more love. Our relationships need more love. Our children need more love. Sometimes, we simple underestimate the power of love and therefore we neglect to use it in every area of our lives and relationships. I'll address love and lovemaking in more detail in a later chapter.

Communications

Communication is the pulse of life. It is our way of showing that we are alive, that we hear, see, smell, taste, and feel. It is the expression of emotions. It is the sharing of thoughts and feelings. It is the lifeline to success, harmony and peace. But silence is also communication.

Lack of communication, miscommunication and harmful communication, are among the biggest causes of divorce. When used appropriately, communication is one of the strongest weapons against divorce and separation. But if used inappropriately, or failing to recognize its importance, it can destroy everything that has been built.

Playwright and economist George Bernard Shaw once said, "The problem with communication… is the illusion that it has been accomplished."

Communication is a constant change. It is one of the pillars that is fluid and must be maintained. We cannot become complacent with communication because it will translate into every other aspect of our relationships. Challenge yourself to improve your personal communication skills and do the same within your relationships. The Bible says in I Cor. 8:2, "Anyone who claims to know all the answers doesn't really know very much." Don't be confused and fall for the illusion that you have already figured out everything that you need to know.

Nelson Mandela said, "If you talk to a man in his language, it goes to his heart." Discover your language. Just like there is a unique love language within a relationship, you need to have a common language when communicating. If you are a combative communicator, chances are you will not get through to a communicator who desires a calm, rational explanation. If your message does not reach your intended audience, it's not communicating. But when it's effective, it reaches and touches the heart.

Benjamin Franklin said, "Tell me and I'll forget. Show me and I might remember. Involve me and I'll understand." Let understanding be your goal in communications. Don't make it about getting your point across or winning an argument. Remember, we are building. Utilize all your senses to communicate and make sure your goal includes giving and receiving understanding.

Roles and Responsibilities

One of the fastest ways to failure is the inability to know, accept, and execute roles and responsibilities. As an avid sports fan, a team's success is predicated on each team member developing his/her skill; learning his/her role; and effectively carrying it out. It's no different in a marriage, or a relationship, or in a home in general.

Just as we bring different experiences to the relationship, we also bring different skill sets that can either help build the relationship or stunt its growth, if we are not willing to come together for the common good of the team. Marriage is a team. Parenting is about teamwork.

When you have clearly identified your goals and have communicated what needs to occur in order to achieve those goals, your roles and responsibilities are your game plan. When team members successfully buy into the game plan, it generally results in team success.

There is no denying that when two individuals come together, they bring different gifts and talents to the table. One might be good at handyman work. The other might be good at cooking. But we can't assume that it's the man who is good at fixing things and the woman who is good at cooking. We bring our assumptions and expectations into relationships and sometimes they blur the game plan. We have to be careful that we are communicating effectively, even as we develop roles and responsibilities. I shouldn't assume that my wife is going to do all the cooking. Maybe she doesn't like to cook. Maybe she can't cook.

So here's what happens. I assume that she's going to do all the cook. When she doesn't, what transpires? When she doesn't, we have conflict in the relationship. What happens when she is placed in that position and she is not effective? We have set the team up to fail, thereby nullifying our goal before we start.

Traditional roles and responsibilities in marriage might

work for some people. The woman cooks, cleans, washes clothes, stays at home and raises the kids. The man works, pays the bills, fixes the broken appliances, and changes the oil in the car. If that works for you, congratulations! Do it! Stick with it! And win with your team! But if tradition doesn't work well in your house, work through it together.

Remember, don't assume or have false expectations based on your background or what you witnessed that you think should happen in your relationships. Communicate with each other and define your own roles and responsibilities. There are several team-building workshops and seminars to help you do that. This is something that can also be discussed in pre-marital and post-marital counseling. If you need help defining roles and responsibilities, don't be afraid to ask. Put aside your pride and always be in team building mode.

Finances

I've never seen a list of reasons for divorce that did not include finances. Check blogs, go to counselors, research online; you will find that money is one of the biggest reasons that marriages and relationships fall apart. Like the fluidity of communication, money constantly changes, usually from your hand somewhere else. When it comes down to it, especially in a marriage, you must be able to figure out what works best and stick with it.

Tarai and I have always shared financial responsibilities in our home. Sometimes, that formula worked perfectly and other times it didn't. Unfortunately for us, we didn't always communicate about the importance of finances, the expectations of finances, or how we perceived the financial responsibilities would play out. As a result, we'd find ourselves disagreeing because one of us thought one thing and the other thought something else. It's something we continue to work on.

Expectations should be clearly defined. All cards should be placed on the table, as they say. Then, devise a plan that works best for you and your household. Don't compare it to the next relationship. Maybe the husband is a professional athlete with millions of dollars on his contract. You can afford to follow the idea that the man is the provider and the woman can be a housewife. But if you were an executive for 10 years before you met your husband, the mechanic, don't assume that you can leave your job and be a housewife the day after you get married and still maintain the quality of life you had living off an executive's salary. I'm not saying you can't do that because you absolutely can. What I am saying is that don't assume that your husband feels the same way. Don't assume that he can afford to do all of the things that you want. Find out. Have those conversations. Find out if making that decision will mean you have lifestyle changes. You might not be able to get your designer shoes as often, or you might have to downgrade from a house to an apartment because that's all you can afford together on one salary, if that is the arrangement.

If you are a team, figure it out together, Find out what's going to make your home, a home sweet home. Whatever you decide, make it work. If it needs to be tweaked along the way, so be it. Just continue building together.

God

Finally, I believe strongly in God as the center of my home and my marriage. But I like to refer to God as the roof, the covering over the pillars and support beams and everything else that goes into the relationship. There is no greater example than that of God and his love for us. I pray that you include God in every aspect of building, whether it's with your spouse or significant other, friend relationships, rearing your children, or at work.

The Bible is a love story. It's a story of redemption. We learn so much about ourselves through our spiritual beliefs, morals, traditions, and experiences. If there is not a degree of commonality as it relates to God, all of the elements from the outside will flood your home and destroy everything that you've built. Amos 3:3 says, "Do two walk together unless they agreed to do so?" There is no bigger issue to agree on than your faith. That should be your foundation *and* your covering.

There are other pillars to successful marriages and relationships. I just wanted to highlight a few. I hope the ones covered help you process them a little easier and that they help your team win.

As we talk about team building and collaborative success, think about these statistics...

- If a baseball player gets a hit 3 out of 10 times at bat, he likely ends up in the baseball hall of fame.
- My favorite basketball team, the Los Angeles Lakers has the highest winning percentage of any professional sports team in American history at

.610, which means they lost 4 out of every 10 games.
- Michael Jordan is arguably the best basketball player to ever play the game, yet he missed more than 9,000 shots in his career, including 26 game-winning shots.

You don't have to be perfect to be successful; you simply have to learn what works best for you and your team and work toward achieving your goals. Don't give up on what works and continue to work on what doesn't.

C. NATHANIEL BROWN

CHAPTER 3
LOVE LESSONS FROM SALSA DANCING

To say I'm not a dancer is an understatement. That guy with two left feet? Yep, I am he! The one black guy without rhythm? Yep, right here! I am the poster child for the Stop Dancin' Movement! I used to be the "wallflower" they talked about at basement parties. I don't even know how to do the Electric Slide, the Cupid Shuffle, the Cha Cha Slide, or any of the other popular line dances. The only time I made it to the dance for was for a little bumping and grinding. Yes, I would slow dance, but even that was off beat. So dancing is not my thing.

But there was something about salsa dancing that piqued my interest. Tarai and I talked about taking a class for years but didn't act on it. Maybe she thought I wasn't serious since she knew about my dancing challenges. We talked about how we could make it a part of one of the activities we did on a regular basis for exercise and to spend time together away from our work, family, church, and other responsibilities. I was serious.

I understand better now that everything happens for a reason and in God's perfect timing. Had we taken a class when we first talked about it, we might have missed the messages we were supposed to receive.

One day, it actually happened. We signed up for an introduction to salsa class. We thought we would learn a few moves, get a little workout, and enjoy spending time with each other in the process. The revelation we received from the first class on continues to blow our minds going on 11 years later. After just a few instructions, we understood that salsa, at least for us, was more than about dancing. We found some parallels between salsa dancing and life; salsa dancing and spiritual growth; and salsa dancing and marriage.

Here are some of the lessons we gleaned from salsa dancing:

- **Lesson 1:** The Man Leads
- **Lesson 2:** The Woman Follows
- **Lesson 3:** Together They Move Gracefully - the grace of the movement comes with the synergy of the man and woman
- **Lesson 4:** The Music Determines the Pace
- **Lesson 5:** Each Gets an Opportunity to Shine
- **Lesson 6:** It Takes Conditioning
- **Lesson 7:** Enjoy the Dance

The Man Leads

The first thing the instructor said was, "The man leads." He said it with conviction and no one in the gymnasium could question his fervor. He had our undivided attention. I was already at a disadvantage. I didn't know how to dance, didn't have confidence in being able to pick up the steps, and quite honestly, I was feeling a little inadequate about my ability to lead in several areas of my life, including with my wife. But the more he talked, the more I zoned in on his every word because I knew there was much for me to learn.

For a while, I had forgotten Tarai was there with me. I was like a child sitting in his favorite class with his teacher introducing a new concept that captivated him. I was committed to getting the message and learning how to dance, even at the expense of embarrassing myself. Sometimes, we have to stare into the mirror and be brutally honest with ourselves if we are going to get better. I was starting from scratch. I could have easily pulled 1,000 excuses from my reserve and backed out. It's not like I hadn't done that before when I felt overwhelmed, overmatched, or overly concerned about the unknown. In those situations, I felt I could save myself some embarrassment, avoid having to work hard, and steer clear of a potential argument or disagreement with my wife. Insert Tarai's assessment of my being passive aggressive. Insert my uncomfortable nature with conflict. But as I listened to the instructor, I was also taking an inventory of my life and hearing that this is something I needed to do. I had to face my inadequacies and insecurities and decide that I was going to learn to salsa dance. I knew the reward would be much greater than the sacrifices I would soon have to make. I had to learn to lead.

The instructor discussed different aspects of salsa basics before showing us any moves. He told us how and where the man held the woman. He demonstrated with his arms the open position and the closed position. "Easy enough," I thought. Then he said you will listen to the beat of the music and begin to count... 1, 2, 3, pause, 4, 5, 6. He repeated it several times. The man starts with his left foot, stepping forward. Still simple enough? Not for me. I was still counting beats. I was starting to feel overwhelmed and I never even attempted one move. But I continued to concentrate as the instructor brought it back to his original point... the man leads.

The way you hold the woman and the way you move your feet and arms dictate what your partner does. "You lead her. You tell her what to do when you move," he said. At that moment, I understood it. Actually, dancing would have been a whole other story at that point but the message stuck. Not only did I hear it clearly, I also understood the bigger picture. I was on board.

The Woman Follows

At that moment, he brought his partner to the center of the circle with him to demonstrate what he just said. As they faced each other, he placed his right arm around her and his hand near the center of her back. With his left, he grabs her right hand and extends it away from their bodies about shoulder high. "The woman follows," he said. Then there was silence. We waited for him to continue. 15 seconds. 30 seconds. A minute.

"What just happened," he asked.

"Nothing," we all replied.

"Exactly! The woman follows so she doesn't move until I move. I lead her to where she is supposed to go," he said.

Ten minutes into our first salsa class and we had a life lesson. I couldn't speak for anyone else at that point but I was being transformed before the music even came on. Since I was getting the bigger revelation, I knew that I would be able to at least limit the embarrassment once we got our chance to follow the instructor's example.

Before Tarai and I married, she was a single mother raising our son. She juggled work, home and church as a minister. She was used to being independent, an alpha woman whom many looked to for personal and career advice. She was a leader. None of that changed after we got married.

In some areas of her life, it actually increased. There's no denying that what she did, she did well. Couple that with her ability to dance and to quickly pick up new dance moves, a potential disaster loomed. It was a bit intimidating because I could imagine her getting upset that she would have to wait on me as I struggled to pick up one or two basic steps. By the time I get those, she could have gone from the beginner to intermediate group. But I didn't bring it up. I knew that if I could embrace the changes I needed to lead, she could embrace the changes she needed to make to follow. I was hoping and praying that it would all fall into place.

Together They Move Gracefully

The music came on and the instructor and his partner demonstrated what he talked us through. He led with his left foot and she stepped back with her right foot. As he brought his foot back, she moved hers forward. He stepped back with his right foot and she put her left foot forward. He stepped to the side and with his arms guided her past him. He lifted her hand above their heads and she twirled around. He grabbed her close and dipped her. We all applauded. It was beautiful. It was simple, yet elegant. It was basic, yet still sexy. The instructor said everything that his partner did was a direct result of what he led her to do. He said if the man leads correctly and the woman follows correctly, it will create the most beautiful dance anyone will ever see. He said the synergy between the man and the woman makes it graceful poetry. I thought, "I'm a poet. I can write poetry. I can do this." I could see myself doing it. I was ready to give it a shot.

And just like that, it was our turn to try it. We got in a circle with our partners. I wasn't nervous as I followed the instructor's demonstration, holding Tarai just like he showed us. He walked us through the moves, slowly, without music. 'Piece of cake,' I thought! We walked through it several times without music. As soon as the music came on, I got intimidated. I tried not to show it but going from slow motion to normal speed trumped my confidence. I didn't give up though. Just as I suspected, Tarai picked it up quickly and was trying to help me get it. She didn't realize how disappointed I was at that moment. I wanted to lead her to this graceful poetry and there she was leading me disguised as helping me.

It was a rocky start. But for my first time dancing, I didn't think it was too bad. I got glimpses of what the dance was supposed to look and feel like. And I liked it. We were working together to make this happen. I was excited.

The Music Determines the Pace

I quickly learned how the music dictates pace of salsa dancing. The beat count remains the same. The exact same moves can be done for slower songs and faster songs. If you learn the basics, you can build upon it. Sounds familiar?

Life happens. Things can go from great to awful in no time. You have to adjust to the beat of life and keep going. In your marriage, there will be times where you don't see eye to eye with your spouse. Don't stop dancing. Find the new rhythm and do the work you know to do. Find out what works and make it happen.

Everybody is different. My preference was for slow salsa music because I could methodically follow the steps that I needed to make. I was trying to make graceful poetry, not play stomp the ants. That's pretty much how it went when the music was too fast for my brain to tell my feet what to do.

Just as conflicting personalities can disrupt relationships, they can do the same on the dance floor. One personality might be fast and the spouse's might be slow. That's the same as the music changing. How do you adjust? What steps do you take to make sure you are bringing that synergy? I'm more laid back than Tarai so sometimes that contributed to our struggles on the dance floor. We weren't dancing to the same music. We've had that happen in our relationship as well where we had to take a step back and ask, "What the heck just happen? How did we get here?" Synching the music is the same thing as getting on the same page. But you both have to be willing to make the adjustments.

I remember the first time I was able to keep up with the faster salsa music. I felt like I had mastered the dance. I knew that if I continued to get better, it would make us both look good. Again, I was willing to adapt to the changes because I wanted the results I believed were possible.

Each Gets an Opportunity to Shine

There were individual things that the man and the woman had to learn in order for the dance to work. But everything to that point was built to create graceful poetry together. But the instructor introduced us to "the shine". A shine is an opportunity within the dance for an individual to showcase dance moves independent of his or her partner.

As I watched the instructor dance with his partner, they each demonstrated a shine. They had their individual personalities on display for 30 seconds or so, twisting, kicking, and shaking. But after that 30 seconds, they came back together and continued that synergetic poetry. It was beautiful. It added another dimension to the lessons I was learning.

I thought about how important it was for Tarai and I to maintain our individual identities and still represent our union to the fullest. That's not always easy to do because so much of who we are as couples is defined by us together. But if we learn to embrace our roles together and determine when it's appropriate to display our individual identities, it makes it easier to come back together after getting our individual shine.

One of the things I love is to support Tarai when she speaks at an event. I like to see her in her element, teaching a class or encouraging someone. I often say, "That girl's good!" And I get that beautiful smile from her. I welcome her times to shine. She is brilliant, beautiful, and wise, independent of me. I would put her accomplishments against anyone's in her areas of specialty, including life coaching, ministry, and parenting. Likewise, I've been able to achieve quite a few successes in my career and ministry, including being a multiple bestselling author, speaking at correctional facilities, and being an award-winning filmmaker. I have no doubt that Tarai is proud of my accomplishments as well. Those are our shines.

Sometimes, life gets us off course. Issues arise, conflicts come, or we just lose our confidence in our spouses or significant others. In other words, the music changes during our shine and we forget (or decide not) to return to our joint dance. Our 30 second shine turns into a weekend of not speaking, which turns into a week, which turns into the door opening to outside distractions and temptations.

We can never forget that if we are a team, we have to remain focused on our goal of winning together and not just our individual accomplishments. That's why I get more excited for those times Tarai and I come back together to continue our dance. As great as we can be as individuals, our greatness is magnified when we are working together. A 30-second shine looks great in the midst of a 4-minute dance with a partner. In most cases, an individual dancing alone, especially salsa dancing, doesn't have that graceful poetic feel.

Get your individual shine and milk it for what it is. But return to your partner to continue to make poetry.

It Takes Conditioning

Tarai took dance classes in college. She's used to dancing. And even though I'm not a dancer, I know what goes into dancing. We expected salsa dancing to be a workout. But neither of us had any idea just how much of a workout it was. After our first class, we felt the burn. We learned that it was only going to get worse when we shifted from primarily slow-motion instruction to full-fledged dancing to fast-paced music. We quickly got there. We understood how important it was to get in shape and stay in shape to dance the way we wanted.

Some salsa songs seem like they go on forever. So think about dancing for hours. It can take a lot out of you physically. But if you are well conditioned, you think less about getting tired and more about your moves and your partner. It takes work to get there and then to stay there.

Once you are there, your dancing shows.

Isn't that the same way with relationships? Sometimes we take for granted the work it takes to have a strong relationship and then to maintain it. We get tired of trying. We get tired of believing. We get tired of fighting. A lot of times we lose focus. If we kept our eyes on the end goal, we'd better prepare to endure the trials and tribulations that ultimately hit most relationships.

What we need to do is concentrate on the areas that exhausts up and build them up. Here's an example to help you understand what I mean. Tarai and I would have a disagreement about something. As we "discuss" the matter, we both shut down because we feel like the other is just not getting it. She knows she's right and she doesn't understand why I just don't see it her way. I know that I am right and can't get why she's being so stubborn. So we'd rather walk away without any resolution because we're both too stubborn to concede anything. In other words, we get tired of going back and forth for what we feel at the time is a pointless journey because neither is going to budge. So our focus is on winning our individual battle rather than coming together so that we win as a team.

So, you can look at this two ways: 1. We did not have the conditioning to stick it out until one of us won; or 2. We had been conditioned to think that nothing would change. Either way, it was a matter of conditioning that needed to be addressed. I'm not going to say we have it all figured out, but we have done a better job of working out many of our issues. You would think that 23 years into a marriage you would have it all figured out. But it takes just as much work now as it did during the early years of our marriage, sometimes more. Physically, I can't play basketball the way I did 23 years ago either. Just like I have to make adjustments in my basketball game, we have to make adjustments in our relationships. We have to locate those areas that typically cause us to tap out, strengthen them, and be more effective moving forward.

I was out of shape when we started salsa classes. I had to work my way back into shape by doing cardio exercises such as jogging, calisthenics, and jumping rope. It made a huge difference as I learned the moves. I was able to dance longer and eventually got a little better with it. In your relationships, you might need to do a heart check. Get in the extra treadmill time or sign up for aerobics. In other words, find out the areas in your relationships that need attention and commit to improving them.

Enjoy the Dance

There are not many dances that are as sexy, entertaining, and fun as salsa dancing. Almost everyone who does it enjoys it. Almost everyone who sees wants to try it. There's just something about it that draws you in. So enjoy it.

The instructor told us that a lot of people wait until they have mastered the dance before they start enjoying it. But he encouraged us to enjoy it along the way. I embraced that. In my quest to get extra practice and get my conditioning in order, I shut myself in my photography studio, turned on YouTube, and danced along with dance instructors from different dance schools. I loved it. I was gradually getting better. The more I learned, the stronger my confidence grew. My conditioning got better. I was enjoying the journey despite not being ready for a real public showing.

I was looking at something I had never tried and I was doing a pretty good job at it. I was still not to the level of Tarai or even many of the others who started the class the same time that we signed up but I was improving. I could look back and see where things were rocky and I could celebrate now being able to spin without losing my beat, put several moves together, and do a shine. This was monumental. But none of that mattered if I wasn't enjoying it.

Of course, I got frustrated sometimes because things change, moves were added that I hadn't practiced and learning to dance with other people sometimes shifted the way Tarai and I danced together. But it was all part of the process. You have your ups and downs but you persevere. There will be things that you won't know or understand but you keep going.

I realized that I had to take that same approach in my marriage and other relationships. It's not always going to be perfect. I'm not always going to understand my wife. I'm not always going to get her to understand me. But I have to understand that it's a part of the journey. I'm going to keep working at it and I'm going to enjoy it along the way. Every opportunity I get to celebrate in the relationships I will. Dance!

C. NATHANIEL BROWN

CHAPTER 4
MAKING LOVE

Before Dark

What's more beautiful than love? Making love?

This book is all about building, strengthening, and maintaining. When it comes to love, it's no different. There is an obvious play on words here as we talk about love and sex. I'm going to address both as we keep consistent with our mission to build.

I love the definitions for 'make' - to form by putting parts together or combining substances; construct; create. The other definition is to cause something to exist or come about; bring about. Isn't that what we've been talking about? Bringing strengths to the table to build a happy home; creating the right atmosphere for stability; and deliberately taking actions to have and maintain strong relationships, are ways that we make love.

Love is a powerful thing. It is the foundation for most of the things that we do and say. So why wouldn't we treat it as delicate and as important as we recognize it to be? Oftentimes we take it for granted just as we sometimes take for granted those our love is meant to benefit.

How many times have you heard, "Love is an action word"? Believe it. Find ways to express your love. Say it. Write it. Text it. Play games. Hide notes in unexpected places. Send flowers just because. Create a date night at home with a picnic on the family room floor (without the family). Find ways to translate love so that it lives. Get it out of your body and out of your mind and into the atmosphere where it can breathe. That's when your spouse will know how much they are loved. And never stop.

For a long time, I've been the friend that others came to for love and relationship advice. I'm not going to say that I had all the answers but I will say that I've been able to help a lot of people with their relationships and marriages. Even before I fully understood God's love and sacrifice for us, I believed in love. I believed in the institution of love. I believe that love works and you can *make* love.

It starts with self-love. We already talked about securing your oxygen mask before assisting someone with their mask. It starts with you. But when you have grasped that love and you extend it to others, it takes on a new life. That person brings another degree of love that multiples yours. It's a beautiful thing. But just as God sacrificed to show his love for us, we must do the same for those we love. That's where we have to commit to making love work. It requires us to look at ourselves, evaluate what we want for ourselves and what we want for the person or people we love. We have to be willing to put in the work to build a love that will weather the storms, so to speak.

When we don't see eye-to-eye on issues, will that love be strong enough to sustain us? Do I trust love enough to invest my all into it with no guarantees that I'll get a return on that investment? We do everything we know to do and still come up short. But as we are constructing what this love is going to be, it requires some blood, sweat and tear equity. Are you willing to make it happen?

I believe the love I have for Tarai is not what it will be when we celebrate our 50th wedding anniversary. I want it to be bigger and better. That doesn't mean that there weren't times when I thought the love had faded and that we should call it quits. That has happened but we always returned to the love and care for each other. We accessed the situations and decided that we would continue to build. It was proof that what we are trying to create is not complete; there is work still to be done. We had to continue to make love.

Never stop loving. Never stop working on your love. If there is ever an endorsement for continuing education, love is it. Continue to learn yourself, continue to learn your spouse and continue to love the process of making it what it should be.

I will be the first to tell you that I'm a lover not a fighter. But there comes a time when you have to be both. You have to fight to gain love and to maintain love. It's ever changing and requires that on-going effort. Some things will come easy and require little to no effort. But then there will be those areas that seem like they just won't cooperate. For example, you might be a cuddler and your spouse might not be. How do you overcome that challenge that you've been facing for years? That can be a major challenge in a relationship. You don't want it to become a stumbling block so you have to continually fight it. And it might be a 15-round heavyweight bout so you have to prepare for it. Train for endurance. Figure out ways to overcome your spouse's objections. Counter with more love. Be a smart fighter. It's not always about strength but how you utilize your skillset to your advantage.

If you approach the situation in a combative way, it will most likely backfire. Yelling and cussing about being neglected and accusing your spouse of having other interests because they don't cuddle can create a greater space between you. Try different approaches. Try asking why they don't cuddle as much. Ask if there's something you can do for them to make it more enjoyable for them. Maybe you can give them a massage and work your way to a cuddle position when they are relaxed. Be creative and be willing to do some things differently than you have in the past. Remember, make love work. Make love work for you, make love work for them, and make love together.

After Dark

On my radio show, The C. Nathaniel Brown Show, my Houston friends Clarence and Tracie White introduced my audience to a 20-day sex challenge that I thought was an awesome idea. They each wrote 10 sexual experiences or fantasies on separate pieces of paper and placed them into a hat or a bag. For 20 consecutive days, they would draw one piece of paper and fulfill what was written on it. It could be a favorite position, a random location in the house, or a fantasy that they never experienced. The idea was to commit to the process, be open to anything, and experience each other in a new, intimate way.

Hasani and Danielle Pettiford, founders of Couples Academy in Atlanta, have what they call the '7 Days of Extraordinary Sex Challenge.' More than 250 couples signed up for the first challenge, which is designed to be an annual effort to help couples connect sexually and emotionally. The Pettifords hope the sex challenge brings passion back into marriages by sharing daily tips, articles, videos blogs and other information to help create excitement for sexual and emotional connections. It turns your attention and energy towards each other, giving you the desire to work through the challenges in your relationship.

For many couples, sex/making love is a taboo issue. It's an uncomfortable topic to discuss. How do you approve such an important building block of marriage when you know it is a sour spot? Return to the building blocks we already covered including reviewing the foundation of the relationship and communicating on an open and honest level with both parties in mind. You can't have a selfish conversation about shared intimacies, or the lack thereof. It has to be team oriented. Make it happen.

When conducting workshops for couples and/or team building, I often use a perspective demonstration where I have two people stand back to back. I ask them to describe what they see in the room. They do and we understand they can only describe what's in front of them. So two individuals in the same room can see two different scenes… perspective.

Have you had an intimate experience with your spouse and you considered it amazing love making and they called it sex? Two people in the same room experiencing one event differently… perspective. What we have to realize in making love, you must understand what a certain experience is for your spouse so that you can accentuate the positives, improve the negatives and win together. That doesn't mean that every time you experience fireworks while making love that your spouse will. It simple means that we have to commit to understand that there is work involved in making sure that both people can appreciate the perspective of the other.

What am I saying? Know what satisfies your husband/wife. Know what satisfies you both. And just like we discussed in the salsa dancing example, figure out how to dance together and enjoy the process.

Remember, what works for another relationship does not necessarily work for yours. So be careful to not allow salon talk or locker room talk to infiltrate your bedroom and create unrealistic expectations. Your best friend might make love to with her husband 20 times a week. But you might bring that expectation home to your husband, who isn't interested or capable of making love to you 20 times a week. Such an unrealistic expectation can create a major strain on your relationship. Rather, find out what works for your relationship. Maybe 10 mutually satisfying times a week is better than 15 disappointments and five average encounters. Find your sweet spot, pun intended. Making love is a great problem to work through. But find a way to figure out what works for you.

Role play. Play games. Experiment. Redefine foreplay. Do what you have to do. In the bedroom, you must find the ingredients to build the love making corridor of your home. Like finances, intimacy in the bedroom can cause a marriage or relationship to crumble. Don't be afraid to spice it up. There are books, videos, blogs, couples groups, etc., that you can use as a basis for exploration. Again, use the process as a way of learning who you are and what you like; who your spouse is and what he/she likes; and what you like together. Be careful not to bring your past experiences, judgements, and relationships into your new bedroom.

Dream Love

Finally, make love in your sleep. I kiss Tarai before she

goes to sleep (usually, I am still up writing) and we say "I love you. Good night." Often, we'll say, "Meet you in my dreams." We always say it when one of us is out of town. But we'll take turns selecting the location. Most times it's "Meet me on the beach (somewhere)." We'll pick another place we have yet to go together like Greece or Belize. It's our way of staying connected and still making love even while we sleep.

It's the little things in building that sustain relationships. So create those intimate moments and opportunities before dark, after dark, and while you sleep. Never stop making love.

CHAPTER 5
EXAMPLES OF LOVE

When I was about four or five years old, I told my mother that I wanted to be a writer. I just knew it. Even at that age, there was something about the ability to express myself with words on the page rather than verbally communicating. Also around the same age, I knew that I wanted to be married and raise a family. I was what the seasoned generations called an old soul.

The irony in wanting to be married was that I had no immediate examples of what marriage looked like. My parents never married. My grandmother was married but was single by the time I was born. None of my aunts or uncles were married. I had one cousin that I remember who got married but I saw them maybe once or twice a year, not nearly enough to understand what marriage was about. There weren't many marriages in my neighborhood either. I could probably count them on one hand and that's saying a lot for a heavily populated community of row houses.

Although I always desired a strong male figure in my life, being raised in a house full of strong, independent women afforded me a lot of advantages. My rationale was they were preparing me for marriage; they thought they were preparing me to be independent, like them.

I never understate what my grandmother, my mother, my aunts and even my female cousins taught me from the time I was old enough to walk. If you can walk, you can push a vacuum, they joked seriously.

They taught me how to cook. I was making my own lunches and taking turns cooking breakfast with my cousins.

I learned to clean. My cousins and I had dishwashing

duties. One would wash, one dried, the other put them away. We had floor sweeping duties, bathroom duties, porch duties, and trash duties. If it had to be done, we did it. I did it.

They taught me how to read and write. My aunt sat my cousins and me and the rest of the neighborhood kids on the steps and taught us to read. We took turns reading and she'd ask us questions to make sure we retained the information. We'd do math problems and have writing exercises. We'd have to share what we learned with one another. We were learning to communicate and implement all that we had been learning.

They taught me respect. I learned how to treat people, especially women. I was taught that chivalry will never die, as long as I was around. I had to open doors for females, be gentle with them, and handle them with care. I asked questions appropriately and answered with respect, saying yes ma'am and yes sir. They taught me the difference in shaking hands with a man versus a woman. They demonstrated how to help a woman down the steps, how to walk on the curb side of the street, and how to be a gentleman.

I gladly soaked up everything. They were teaching me about life as they knew it and I was thinking about how I would one day treat my wife. As I took it all in, I knew all these things would help me down the road.

Tarai, on the other hand, grew up with both parents in the home. I am in no way saying my in-laws had the perfect marriage or that they didn't have issues as an individual man and an individual woman. But Tarai had a different experience from mine. Yes, she learned a lot of the same things I did about cooking and cleaning and responsibilities. As an older sister, she even had to be the protector and defender, much like I had to be for my younger and older cousins. She had people there who supported her and made sure she had life's necessities for a child – food, shelter, love and a chance. We both did. But she also had an example of a husband and a wife. On a daily basis, she could watch the building of a relationship, the raising of a family, the roles of husband and wife being defined right before her eyes. Whether what she was witnessing was the perfect example or worst example, isn't the important factor to me; she had an example that helped shape her ethos.

We often wondered how much that factored into some of our difficult times. Did I penalize her because she didn't measure up to my non-example image of what my wife would be? Did she penalize me because I didn't say or do something the way her dad said or did something for her mother? Did the lessons she learned make her feel that her way is not only right but the only way? Were my lessons shaping the way I treated her as if she never had a man involved in her life? Were our definitions of vital terms so different that it caused rifts? What is protection? What is support? What does respect look like to you?

Sometimes, we learn expectations based on our upbringing and our environments. Our behavior is based on what we witness from our parents, our extended family members, our friends' families, our communities, and everything we see around us, consciously and subconsciously. We learn by seeing and doing. That's why as kids we repeat things we hear and follow people around imitating them. We acquire good and bad habits that way. As we will discuss in a later chapter, it's also how we shape our understanding of roles and responsibilities in marriage.

Because I was on a quest for marriage, I also watched couples and marriages on television and in the movies trying to understand this phenomenon I had no direct connection to. I also had my fair share of experiences with girlfriends and crushes along the way, trying to implement the things I learned from home and afar. I beamed with pride when girls used to tell me how much of a gentleman I was and how I was different from other guys. I knew that the women in my family did a great job.

But there are still some things that I missed, not having a man around to teach me things from a man's perspective. My aunt taught me how to throw a left jab, followed by a right cross and an uppercut. She taught me how to defend myself against a bully by punching him in the solar plexus and kneeing him in the head when he bent over. And they all made sure I protected my female cousins in the neighborhood, even though I was much smaller than most of the kids. As great of a job I think they did in raising me, I still believe I missed a lot by not having a strong man around and a strong man married to a strong woman. As a result, I believe that may have contributed to some issues in my marriage to a strong woman.

Yes, there are some things that all women desire such as respect, strength, protection, and security. There are some things that all men want such as respect, support, to be wanted and needed, and love. But just as every man is different, every woman is different. You have to be flexible enough to know what you know and adapt to what you need to know. Everything that is good to you is not good for you, I heard someone say. I continually have to evaluate how what I know impacts what goes on in marriage or relationships in general. I have to be flexible enough to switch things up to make them work in that relationship. Likewise, my wife, or the other party in the relationship, must be willing to do the same.

Oftentimes, we learn to do things one way and we know it works and is right. But there are more than one way to cook chicken. Be willing to learn new recipes and you could learn a lot about yourself, others and more importantly about your team.

Unfortunately, we get stuck in our ways and are more concerned with being right or getting the last word than coming together and being a successful team. You can be right and still lose. Marriages are about winning together. TEAMWORK - Together Everyone Achieves More!

Tarai and I have a special thing we do. Let's say she calls me to help her move something. We coordinate, give our count… 1-2-3, and lift. We move the object and when we're done, we give each other a hi-five and say, "Teamwork!" It can seem so insignificant until you experience lonely times, even in your marriage. You feel like you can't get help with simple things that would make your life so much better. Anger builds. Disappointment enters. You get frustrated and feel like being spiteful. And it all happens because that teamwork isn't there when you feel you need it. It happens. You have your good days and you have your bad days. No one is perfect, even though we all think we are sometimes. The bottom line is we have to limit the times when we abandon the team for whatever reason. When you train yourself to focus on team, you are more willing to sacrifice so that everyone achieves more. The more we win, the less we'll allow opportunities to arise that will halt that momentum. And when you win, celebrate!

That's why when I look back on all the work my cousins and I had to do as kids, I can appreciate it more. I realized all the lessons we were learning about working together, about achieving a common goal, and enjoying the success together, were a part of a great foundation.

But on August 12, 1995, I also realized I still had so much to learn. That was the day Tarai and I got married. All the preparation, practice, and pursuit was over; it was game time. I had to try to apply everything I learned through my family, television, movies, the few marriages in my community, and the ones I watched as I matriculated through college and after college. I knew I was going up against a formidable opponent, but I was confident because I had my life partner, my teammate with me. I was fearless and believed that nothing would be able to stand up against us. Besides, I was practically born for this and she was game. As smart as we were as individuals, I knew we could handle anything together. It didn't matter that more than half of marriages ended in divorce. Team Brown was going to win! It didn't matter that I never had a successful marriage in my family. Team Brown was going to be the standard! It didn't matter that there were and would be naysayers. Team Brown was going to win!

With all that, I didn't realize how much we had to learn about each other, our pasts, and how much we would have to grow in order to be successful as a team. And that's what we set out to do.

CHAPTER 6
FAMILY AND FRIENDS

There's nothing like having the support of family and friends when you are trying to build a marriage, raise a family, establish a business, or promote a product or service. But as they say with anything, too much of a good thing can become a bad thing.

Be careful of the level of involvement you allow from family and friends, especially in your marriage and relationships where they only have a cursory view. We all have relatives and friends who think they know everything. We know they have to be pretty intelligent to be connected to us, but we also must know that we all have our issues and sometimes minding *your* business is not the business they should be concerned with.

The saying goes, "keep your friends close and your enemies closer..." so you can look out for them. But, just as you keep haters away from your relationships, there are times when you have to do the same for family members and friends even though they mean well.

Family and friends' roles are very important in the building process. They obviously have your best interest at heart (usually). They want to see you happy. They want to see you win. They don't want to see you hurt. They don't want to see you fail. So what happens if you are unhappy? Usually, it impacts everyone around you, including them. So, they have vested interest in your success. If family and friend relationships are built using the same model of a strong foundation with strong support beams, and important ingredients inside to personalize it, it should be about teamwork and everyone succeeding.

Family and friends should be your support system. Those who are married and have experience dealing with issues that you never faced are excellent sources of wisdom. They can help you understand how different things are once you are married, how there is a greater commitment required, and how everything you do has a greater impact on others, especially if there are children involved.

When we are newly in love or recently married, we fall into that newlywed mode where all our happiness is wrapped up in our significant other. It's about love, feelings and emotions. We just want to spend time together, sharing every moment gazing into each other's eyes, counting stars together and planning out fantasies. It's what we do and we love it. But we all know that subsides at some point. You don't stop loving each other but the reality is you return from fantasy land to discover that bills are due; you have to get your credit right to purchase a house; you have kids and now have to deal with daycare; you have arguments about a picture on social media; you fight about spending habits; you don't like him/her spending so much time with their friends; and you just want some space away from them. Your support system should be there to help you navigate through the murky waters and figure out what's at the core of the issues so you can return to that happy place.

An experienced couple can share their experiences going through similar situations to let you know you are not dealing with an isolated incident. Your situations and circumstances might be different, but you'll learn that many couples have similar issues that can be overcome. That type of advice is priceless. But you want to make sure that you go to pro-marriage family members and friends with that type of experience. Avoid those who have been jaded by their experiences and don't want to see anyone happy. They will try to get you to walk away from your happiness because of minor issues. They will say something like, "It only gets worse from here," or "You're better off just leaving her now."

Remember our mindset should always be to build. If your family and friends are truly on your side, that's what their intentions should be. That doesn't mean they will always tell you warm and fuzzy things, but they will tell you the ugly truth with love.

I had a conversation with my mother in-law about a rocky time in my marriage to her daughter. Not only was she one of my biggest cheerleaders and supporters and wanted to make sure that her daughter was happy, but she had been married for 25-plus years at the time of this conversation. I started venting to her, as we do when we are emotionally frustrated. A big part of me just wanted her to take my side and tell me that I was right and her daughter was wrong. I wanted that validation that I had a right to be pissed off. With very little emotion, she sat there and listened to me vent. When I was done, she looked me right in the eyes, put her hand on my knee and said, "Now, what are you going to do to make this right?"

I was a taken aback. Maybe she didn't understand that I was coming to her complaining about things I felt my wife was doing to make me angry. I wanted to hear her say, "You're right! She is being a jerk and she needs to get it together." Whether that was the case or not, my mother in-law looked beyond my emotional tirade and got to the core of the matter. She made me look at my role in the matter. It wasn't about being right or wrong; it was about getting right from a wrong situation and it started with me.

Sure, there have been times when I went to my mother in-law, or my mother, or my best friends and explained what I was going through or what I was feeling and they sided with me. They told me I was justified in feeling the way I did and that my wife was wrong. Sometimes, all I needed was to vent and hear that I was right. But the friends and family who love you will also tell you when you are wrong. Their intentions, either way, should be to support you and help you get back to a healthy relationship. You should expect that from them and they should expect that from you.

Be careful what you share and to whom you share it. Everybody doesn't need to know all your business. Sometimes, the ones you feel have your back will be the ones who use the information you share against you or your relationship. Obviously, these aren't the people you want in your circle but sometimes we don't learn that until it's too late.

I had a friend who shared with another friend personal information about difficult times he was having with his wife. They talked about how the wife felt insecure about her husband's friendship with a woman whom he had no intimate relations. The husband shared how his wife was jealous of this woman and wanted more of his attention as a way of keeping him away from this woman or any other woman. But the friction in their relationship distanced the husband and the wife assumed he was spending this time with other women. The so-called friend used that information to plant more insecurities in the woman's mind by saying that he and the husband had been to several nightclubs together. He also played on the wife's emotions in an attempt to slither his way in while the husband was away.

His plot failed. Needless to say, the men were no longer friends and fortunately the couple were able to overcome their issues and remain married.

During a difficult time in a marriage of a couple I counseled, the wife shared with her family the struggles she and her husband were having including his being unfaithful. They were considering divorce but also contemplating if the marriage was salvageable. The wife's family became irate and immediately turned against the husband, calling him everything but a child of God. He became to them an enemy, even though the wife said they were still considering reconciling. They did try to make things work but every time he was around, you could feel the tension in the room. He was aware that they knew of the difficult times he and his wife dealt with but he didn't know she told them about his infidelity. At one point, they were so supportive of him but now they were cold. When they finally discussed how he felt around her family, she told him they knew about what had happened.

He was irate. He questioned her about why she shared their business. She explained that she was lost and hurt and needed someone to talk to so she went to her aunt whom she trusted. From there, the conversations went to cousins who consoled her. She explained how much it helped her with her feelings and emotions. The husband asked her one question, "Did you tell them that you had been unfaithful to me before that?" Her answer was no.

You have to be careful what information you share, how much information you share, to whom you share the information, and consider the impact sharing the information can have. Unfortunately, that couple's marriage ended in divorce. I can't say for sure if that incident is what did it but there were a lot of issues they couldn't resolve and family and friends' involvement had a big role in it.

When it comes to parenting, family and friends can be a big help. They can offer childrearing advice, babysit, and share best case practices to help build your home. Sometimes it's the small things family and friends do that have the biggest impact; it's not always about offering the life-changing advice or coming to your defense with a Smith and Wesson handgun. Watching the kids so you and your spouse can have a date night goes a long way in building a healthy marriage. That two-hour getaway can take you back into fantasy land just long enough to give you the energy needed to get through a difficult time later.

But don't overlook the Smith and Wesson moments either. If anyone has your back, it should be family and friends. They should be standing by you and with you during the toughest times of your life. If that means going into battle, so be it. The same ones who will lift you up and champion you and the same ones who will give you the cold, hard truth when you need it, should be the same ones willing to go into the trenches with you. They are there during late nights at the emergency room when the kids are sick and God forbid, bailing you out of jail when things go haywire.

Unfortunately, that's doesn't always happen. In difficult times, you really find out who is for you and who is against you. The same ones who support you when things are going well, are often the same ones who bail on you when you need them most. You know the ones who never have money when you are in a financial crisis or the ones who never have time for you despite always calling on you when they need something? So you have to take the good with the bad and determine who will be your true support system to help you build. If they can't measure up, they have to go (or at least stay far enough away as to not hinder your building process).

Unfortunately, you will have to let some family members and friends go. When they try to run your life opposed to supporting your life, you need to create space. When you don't have to, don't make it a permanent move or one that is unrepairable. But you have to make your point that your life is just that... your life. Explain to them that you are building a family, building a relationship or building a home and their involvement is stunting that growth. Be sure to let them know that you appreciate their love and support but you have to figure some things out on your own. Ask them to respect that decision and not give up on you and your relationship with them. Sometimes this can be a difficult situation. Depending on how you express yourself and how they receive it, it can go over very well. But it can also turn into an ugly fight that ends that relationship. If you have done everything right and in love, they should respect it and be with you through thick and thin. If they don't, maybe they were not supposed to be a part of your support team moving forward.

C. NATHANIEL BROWN

CHAPTER 7
CHILDREARING

Childrearing, AKA parenting, is a total team effort that impacts everyone involved. It's not easy, sometimes simply difficult, but the importance of doing it right cannot be underestimated. We've all seen individuals who seem like they just can't stay out of trouble. It could be a child actor, an athlete, or someone from your community. Oftentimes we wonder if the way the child was raised played a part in the decisions they made later in life. Sometimes, that is the case and other times in might just be bad decisions that are unrelated to anything a parent did or didn't do.

In cases of physical, emotion, and sexual abuse, we seem to understand when those children grow up and act out the pain they experienced. It doesn't excuse it but we understand in those situations how parents can fail their children. But what about other parents, such as those who don't care or the ones who just don't know how to raise their children? They fail them as well.

It is everybody's responsibility to raise children. Someone once said, if you know better, you do better. It starts at home and should extend to every facet of our lives including our extended families and friends, in schools, in churches, and in the community.

Tarai and I took childrearing seriously. But just as we discussed earlier, it involves so much more than a simple list of dos and don'ts. We bring all of our experiences and beliefs with us into parenting and that can positively and negatively impact the home.

I want to cover five areas that are important in childrearing and how we dealt with them in raising our son and my daughter (from a previous relationship). They are grown now and I believe we did a pretty good job. I hope our experiences help others navigate through the processes for their own homes. Remember, that every situation is different and I'm not suggesting anything I say to be the iron clad law. But if something I share helps you, by all means utilize it. It's about learning, growing, and building.

Instill Morals and Values

Tarai and I were raised in different family structures but we both were raised with certain morals and values that we believed attracted us to each other. Her parents and my mother and the women of my family taught us things such as respecting elders, how to treat people, how to take care of ourselves, the importance of religion, and strong family bonds. Some things we learned on our own through life experiences, hard knock lessons, and life in general. So when we came together to raise a family, we had to figure out some things that would help us successfully instill the right morals and values that would ultimately produce quality adults.

It wasn't always easy because in addition to learning how to parent together, we were also learning to live as husband and wife. But we had a strong foundation on which to build. We knew that we wanted to raise our children with the fear and admonition of God; we wanted them to be respectful; and we wanted them to have a better childhood experience than we (although we were raised well).

I shared in my book, Devil in the Mirror: Overcoming the Enemy's Attack, how I used to tell my son to 'represent', which meant to represent God, represent family, and represent himself in a stellar manner. It was something we said which spelled out a lot of unspoken instructions based on morals and values. We understood it, even when we fell short sometimes. But it became our constant gauge to help us line up with what mattered most to us as a family and the lives we wanted to live.

When families seemed to become so isolated with mom and dad working all the time and children in so many activities or consumed with video games and electronic devices, family meal time somehow lost its significance. But Tarai and I wanted family meals to remain a strong fabric of our makeup as Team Brown. We took time to share those family moments over a meal. It was also a time just to talk. You learn so many things about one another just by slowing down and talking *and* listening.

We also set aside time for family fun, game nights, and family outings. It emphasized the importance of family and letting the children know that no matter how busy or chaotic things are, we make time for one another. You have no idea the impression a family movie makes. What a child gets from laughing with his/her parents playing a board game is immeasurable.

Introduce Traditions

Those times set aside for family become traditions. Growing up, we had so many family traditions that I can't possibly share them all. But they meant the world to me. Whether it was holiday traditions such as decorating the Christmas tree or getting new clothes for Easter, or picking greens with my grandmother. Tarai and I wanted to continue some traditions like each person opening one present on Christmas Eve. We also wanted to start new traditions that were unique to us.

We were never what you would consider rich, but we understood that we were more fortunate than a lot of people. So we made sure we gave to the less fortunate. We'd regularly go through our wardrobes and collect clothes we no longer wore and donated them to shelters, homeless ministries and the Goodwill. We wanted to instill a sense of humility and service in our children. We wanted them to know that they might not have everything that they want, but they have plenty.

I also never took for granted the privilege I had of teaching my children the importance of praying before they went to bed. I didn't have many pleasures as rewarding as tucking my children in at night, kissing them and telling them that I love them. Sometimes, we take things like that for granted but it's a powerful impact for a child to know their parents love and care for them.

So, find ways to create traditions that have long-term impact on your family and develop character at the same time. It goes a long way in building a strong family for generations. Your children will appreciate it and pass them down to their children as well.

Discipline

How you discipline your children is always a hot topic in our society, especially these days when kids are divorcing their parents and Children and Youth Services get involved with the slightest disciplinary actions by parents. Our parents and grandparents would have still been in jail if they were governed by today's discipline standards. Almost everything is considered child abuse.

Tarai and I had various approaches to disciplining our children. And we didn't always agree with the punishment or the length of the punishment. But to the best of our abilities, we tried to show a united front, even though we knew they would try to pit one against the other. Oftentimes, we'd used that to our advantage.

We'd play good cop/bad cop. I was/am a softee when it comes to my kids. I'm like putty in their hands. It was difficult for me to separate my love and adoration for them and discipline then. Tarai, on the other hand, was a stern disciplinarian. She was the primary disciplinarian despite my failed attempts to bail the kids out of trouble. Sometimes, we used that to our advantage. I'd play the good cop trying to make sure I explained everything that happened and get their explanations. Tarai would come in and drop the hammer. It wasn't always easy because we didn't always agree. But we stayed united and made it work.

In typical kid fashion, they'd try to pit us against each other whenever they could. But we quickly saw through their plans most of the time. If I told one of them they couldn't do something, they'd go behind my back to see if Tarai would let them before I found out. But she'd ask, "Did you ask your dad? What did he say?" In most cases, they would fess up. They just hoped one of us didn't ask what the other said.

Tarai also used the threat of telling me what they did. As soft as I was to them, they knew that if I had to discipline them it was going to be serious. Tarai would say, "Wait to your dad gets home. I'm gonna tell him what you did." They would quickly try to make amends with her before I got home. Or she'd ask, "Do you want me to tell your dad?" They would say no.

Even though I got whooped with belts, switches from trees, hands and anything else that was close enough to use, I never wanted to discipline my children that way. I have smacked their hands and their butts, more to scare them than anything. But they did have privileges revoked, extracurricular activities taken away and extra chores. We tried to stress the lessons with every act of discipline so they would learn from it and not make the same mistakes. Of course, that was hit and miss as well (no pun intended this time). But our goals for them remained to develop them into intelligent, talented, upstanding citizens with good morals and values. Discipline helped in that process.

Dealing with Unique Issues

We had some very interesting issues that we dealt with as a family. Tarai served as a single mother for nearly four years of our son's life before she and I got married. So, there were certain things that we married within our relationship as parents together. As I mentioned, our discipline methods were different so I had to get used to her paint stirrer-turned whoopin' stick and she had to get used to my alternative approaches including a good talking, too. It sounds a little comical but there were adjustments that needed to be made. We also had to figure out other things we could do to accomplish the same goals. That involved sacrificing some of our own thoughts and beliefs to compromise and work as a team.

Not only were Tarai and I learning each other as we were becoming one, our son was learning a lot, too. He had to learn how to be a son to a father he didn't really know. He had to share his mother for the first time in his life. He had to figure out what his parents' new lives meant to his young world. So, Tarai and I had even more responsibility to make sure what we were building helped all of us. It didn't come without challenges, but we figured out how to make things work. I learned some things from her and she learned some things from me. That made it easier for us to teach our son all the things that he would need to grow into the man we prayed for him to be.

In a similar manner, we had to deal with my daughter when she came to visit some holidays but primarily during the summer. She is two years older than my son but she had to deal with many of the same adjustments. She was used to it just being her and me. But now she had to deal with sharing me with Tarai and her brother. And we had to deal with making sure we limited the tension. What was Tarai and my daughter's relationship going to be without my involvement? What would she call her? How would they get along? We tried to avoid the 'step' titles because we wanted to just be a family but sometimes it became awkward. Other times, Tarai felt that I disciplined my son more than I disciplined my daughter for similar transgressions. So again, we had to come up with ways of sifting through the issues and correct them for the sake of the team.

The kids were amazing together, as if they lived together all of their lives. I think we did a good job of making sure they felt comfortable around each other but they had a natural chemistry without us.

During her senior year of high school, my daughter lived with us in Pittsburgh. It is what I called the greatest year of my life because I had my family all together and not just for a long weekend or summer break. But that presented problems, too, because we all had to re-learn some things. But overall we figured out how to make things work.

Blended families can create a lot of challenges but committed families overcome them. We were committed. We still are committed.

Impact of Parents and Their Relationship

Raising children is not easy. It requires a lot of time, commitment, energy, know-how, patience, discipline, and so much more. And that's just the parents to children. What about the impact childrearing has on the parents' relationship? If the parents are divided on issues such as discipline, education, morals and values, and religious beliefs, it can create an enormous strain on the parent's relationship. Many marriages have ended in divorce because of the inability to co-parent.

It hasn't always been peaches and cream between Tarai and me and sometimes it has been because of disagreements when it came to the children. Maybe it was a disciplinary issue or the feeling like one or the other didn't fulfill parenting expectations. Who was supposed to pick him up from school? Why did you let them do that after I told them they couldn't? As with any argument, it has the potential to go on for days or weeks if left unresolved.

We tried our best to limit those situations. Sometimes, we were successful and other times not so much. But what we tried to do is make sure that we carved out time for ourselves and spent time trying to build our relationship the same way we were trying to build the children. We took our son to grandma's house and had date night. Sometimes we chose to talk about parenting type issues and other times we agreed not to talk about anything except us – no homework, no afterschool program, no disciplinary actions... only adult content. It worked.

So parents have to remember themselves and their spouses in the midst of raising the children. Everybody should be in a state of growth. Find ways to create balance because a balanced life produces fruit. Don't forget... "Living things grow and growing things live." So if you are not growing and living, you are withering away and dying. We see a lot of marriages fall apart for that exact reason.

Now that we are empty nesters, we can look back and be proud of the job we did raising two phenomenal adults. But we can also be just as proud that we were able to overcome all of the challenges that came against us to do a good job for them and for our marriage.

Bonus Story

Daddy Kisses

Like me, my son was what we called an old soul at a young age. He was mature for his age and discussed things like an adult. He had a lot of things figured out that somewhat baffled me, but not too much being that I was similar.

When he was about four years old, we used to wrestle. I'd let him get the best of me for a short period before I flipped him over and started kissing him on his face, neck and head. He would get the biggest thrill out of it and laugh uncontrollably. So every night when I would tuck him in, I'd give him a kiss and tell him I loved him.

Well, my son would always blush when Tarai and I kissed him and didn't like us to kiss him in public. One day, I caught on to something he did at home. He'd be lying in the bed or on the couch with a blanket and all of a sudden he'd throw the blanket over his head and start yelling, "Don't kiss me! Don't get me!" That was my cue to start wrestling him and giving him daddy kisses. It was the sweetest thing in the world. It was one of those subtle messages that I was fortunate enough to pick up on that whenever it happened, it made both of our worlds.

My wife is no different. One day, she said something sarcastic like only she can. When she saw the reaction on my face, she laughed and ran into the other room. So I chased her, laid on top of her on the couch, and started tickling her and kissing all over her. She laughed so hard that tears fell from her eyes and she yelled that she had to go to the bathroom. It was one of those perfect moments.

Sometime later, she told me she loved when I chased her, much like my son throwing that blanket over his head and telling me not to kiss him. So I picked up on it, not just because I'm that in tune with everything but because it was familiar and there are not many things in the world that I enjoy more than seeing the people I love laugh and smile.

So there were many times that she'd say something to me that I didn't pick up on her hint until I saw her look back over her shoulder like, 'Come get me, Daddy!" When she saw I got it, she'd move just fast enough to cue me to chase her. And I obliged.

At the time of this writing, I have a fresh example to share with you. She and I have this ongoing joke about we are not the boss of the other. I told her that we were going to do something and she said to me, "You're not the boss of me!" This is nothing new because we say that to each other all the time. But this time she looks back over her shoulder and I knew.

My daughter, on the other hand, was a little different. She loved my kisses. She loved kissing her daddy. But I had to learn her 'thing'. Well, I used to sing a song I made up that I sang as I rocked her in my arms. After she got too big to throw in the air and bounce on my shoulders, I stopped singing the song. One day, we went to the park and as I was pushing her on the swing, she asked me, "Daddy, why don't you like to sing anymore?" It hit me like a ton of bricks. The only time I ever sang was when I sang to her. I knew that she wanted me to sing *her* song. So I did. After that, I made sure I looked for my cue to sing her song.

The moral of the story is… pay attention to the signs. The little signs and the big signs are designed to help you navigate to your destination. At the same time, it will bring joy to the lives of the ones you love. So listen intently and make it a point to deliver. It may be that child calling out for love, affection, or affirmation. Or it could be your spouse looking back over his/her shoulder and you know that all signs say it's a go.

C. NATHANIEL BROWN

CHAPTER 8
COUNSELING

Pre-Marital Counseling

When I was 24 years old, I had two children and was about to marry my son's mother. What did I know about being married other than I knew since I was a kid that I wanted to be married and raise a family. Tarai and I met with the pastor of the church we attended about preparations for the August 12, 1995, ceremony. Who would sing what? What scriptures would be read? What music would the bridesmaids walk down the aisle to? Then the discussion turned to premarital counsel.

Tarai and I had briefly discussed it. Even though I didn't have examples of marriages I could turn to and Tarai had her parents to look to, we weren't quite on the same page about counseling. We both thought we were smart enough that we really didn't need it, but I thought it could only help. Eventually, we agreed to go through with it. We didn't really know what to expect but we wanted to be open.

I don't remember how many sessions we had with Pastor Roger Thomas, but I know that we didn't get many life-altering lessons from it. I was glad to hear about his experiences with his wife and his family, some references to marriage from the Bible, and a few nuggets about making sure we always dated. As a relatively new born-again Christian, I appreciated the experience of sitting down with an elder who wanted the best for me and my family.

It was during premarital counseling that Pastor Thomas first mentioned the ingredients coming together to make a cake and how leaving out ingredients can alter the taste of the cake. It's the blending of the appropriate portions of the ingredients that makes the cake turn out the way it was intended. During our wedding ceremony, he used the story to charge us as a couple by saying we are bringing unique gifts and talents together to create a marriage that will be an example to many others. I held onto that message.

Years later, Tarai and I wondered what else we could have dealt with during premarital counseling that might have helped us avoid some of the difficulties in our marriage. We agreed that premarital counseling is a proactive approach to planning, building and maintaining a strong and healthy relationship. If marriage is to be a union that is meant to last a lifetime, this counseling, whether it's a 6-week or 6-month training, would help remove some of the emotion from being engaged; get to the heart of marriage matters; learn what helps build a healthy marriage; identify common stumbling blocks in marriages; and learn how to always work as a team. So we identified several areas and implemented them into our counseling as ministers to help other couples, especially during premarital counseling.

If it's true that couples who participated in premarital counseling is less likely to divorce, it's something that more people should consider.

Below are nine of the key topics that should be covered during premarital counseling:

- Love
- Finances
- Children/Family
- Sex/Intimacy/Dating
- Family/Friends

- Religion/Spirituality
- Roles and Responsibilities
- Planning/Problem Solving (identifying stressors)
- Maintaining Your Identity

Love

A man meets a woman, wines and dines her, and wants to get to know her better. The woman believes she's found her knight in shining armor, the one she's been praying for since she was playing house as a kid. They spend every possible hour together falling in love. He eventually proposes and she gladly accepts. They are on their way to eternal happiness, right?

Well, love is one of the areas to talk about before they get to the altar and exchange vows. The novelty of meeting someone who has the characteristics you've been looking for will eventually wear off. Having that feeling of a high school kid dating again wears off. The missing someone for a few days because your work schedules won't allow you to see each other wears off when you live together. The family issues finally arrive now that you have put your guard down. Now what?

Counseling can help you discover your partner's definition of love, why it is important, and what examples he/she holds onto as a reference to loving others. Love is the foundation because it provides you with the basis to deal with everything else in a relationship.

You hear people say, "I love you but I'm not in love with you." Couples need to understand what statements like this mean to their partner. When someone says they love you, what does that really mean? It's a discussion that many couples overlook because they believe that once they say they love each other, everything else will fall into place. That's when we become complacent and allow so many issues to creep in. Premarital counseling is a great time to have that discussion if it wasn't already had.

Finances

People still get funny over money. It remains one of the most difficult topics for couples to discuss. Despite agreeing to join together in holy matrimony, many couples still believe that talking finances is taboo. Some believe that it's the man's role to handle all of the financial matters in the relationship and any money the woman makes is for her to use at her discretion. Others believe they should put all of their money in a joint account and all decisions related to that money needs to be discussed and agreed upon. Others have some version of financial management based on their beliefs, traditions, and people in their ears telling them "what supposed to be".

Unfortunately, a lot of couples don't have this discussion until after they are married and living under the same roof. They bring up their individual expectations and understanding of handling financial matters and it creates a disagreement because the other partner thought they were on the same page.

Counseling might not solve every problem a couple has for the rest of their lives, but it can develop a game plan that the team can start off following. That will give them a firm foundation of understanding on matters such as who pays what and what happens in cases of emergency. If at some point adjustments need to be made, they can do that and they'll have a basis for how to have those discussions.

These sessions are also a great opportunity to find out about your partners spending habits, if they can save money, and what their current credit situation is. Some people are afraid to discuss those issues with fears of jeopardizing the relationship. But bad credit and the inability to purchase your dream home because of bad credit can jeopardize the relationship as well.

Finding out disturbing information about finances during counseling sessions doesn't mean an end to the relationship; it simply means that you are aware of what you will be dealing with once you are married. However, if it is a red flag or one of your 'deal breakers' then you will have learned the information before stating "until death do you part".

Children/Family

By the time most couples agree to marry, they have already discussed family, how many children they want, and what their vision is for their family. But that's not always the case. I talked to a couple whose marriage was in dire straits because they didn't know the other's expectations about family. The husband wanted children and the wife didn't so you can imagine the strife and tension that existed whenever the topic came up.

Family is usually an easy topic to discuss, even without a counselor. But there are also situations that can make it difficult. For example, if the woman has had a hysterectomy and can't have children, she might not be comfortable talking about it for fear of her partner rejecting her. Maybe the man doesn't want children and is afraid to share that because he doesn't want the woman to feel like it's because of her.

Children and family need to be discussed. The sooner that discussion takes place, the easier it will be to build the relationship and family. Don't be afraid to have the difficult discussions early. They save a lot of heartache and pain down the road.

Sex/Intimacy/Dating

Do you know your partner's opinions about dating? What is his/her definition of intimacy? How important is sex to him/her? Do they need it 3-5 times a week or is once a month sufficient? What about oral sex? Is anything taboo? Are we going to have date nights? What is considered romantic?

For some people, asking these questions are a no-brainer. It comes with the territory and is to be expected among your normal conversations. But that's not the case for everyone. During counseling sessions, asking and answering these questions can be done in a variety of ways to make it fun and interesting and to break the barriers so you can get to the heart of the matter.

We know that the answers to some of these questions can be deal breakers but people still refuse to have the conversations. It should be covered in premarital counseling so the couple can have an idea of what to expect from their partner. Men and women have extramarital affairs because they don't receive at home what they expected. They seek outside of the marriage what they feel they are missing inside, causing tremendous pain in the relationship. In many cases, this can be avoided by having the discussions before the wedding.

Family/Friends Involvement

There are many questions that need to be asked about the role of family and friends in relationships. Sometimes people assume that their relationship with their family is the same kind of relationship between their partner and their families. How many times has that been false? What's going to be friend time? How often do the boys hang out? Will there be a houseful of guests all the time? What type of friends are they? Friends have roles in relationships as well and sometimes they are more involved than family members because people usually share intimate details of their relationships with a best friend. Is this best friend someone who can be trusted? Do they have the marriage's best interest or will they be so loyal to the friend that they won't allow the relationship to grow?

You also will want to look at family history to determine what type of generational issues are in the family genealogy. Are there genetic issues that will effect having children? Is there a history of mental health issues or domestic violence? Are there criminal elements that need to be avoided? Are there family members that would be out to sabotage the relationship? Again, some of the areas may be difficult to discuss during a dinner date but in the atmosphere of a counseling session, they can be easier to dissect.

Religion/Spirituality

What role will religion and spirituality play in your marriage? Is it going to be a house of faith or are you going to avoid any religious activities? Are you going to celebrate holidays? Will the children believe in Santa or will Christmas be strictly about the birth of Jesus Christ? What are your thoughts on idolatry? Are we going to regularly attend church, a mosque, mass, or some other religious gathering?

Little things give us a sense of security and we easily assume something that might not be our reality. At dinner, we see our partner praying over his food. We assume he is praying to the same God that we prayed to. But it could be something totally different. He/she could be praying to the animal that was sacrificed for them to have nourishment.

Common religious beliefs can provide a level of comfort and stability when building a relationship and family. But conflicting views create a holy war within a marriage. The Bible says two people can't walk together unless they are on the page. There is no bigger gap in pages than to be on opposite sides of religious and spiritual views.

Roles and Responsibilities

There aren't many areas of a marriage that create drama more than roles and responsibilities. We have built-in expectations of what roles our spouse should play. They come from the marriages we see around us, marriages on television and the movies, and what we fantasized about for years. But the truth of the matter is that our spouses might have something different in mind. If the roles and responsibilities are not discussed, we bring those assumptions and expectations into the marriage and the minute that they are not fulfilled, there is a major problem. But if they were discussed ahead of time, everyone would be on the same page and the only disappointment will be when they are not done but not because they didn't know and agree to do them.

When discussing roles and responsibilities, it should always be been done from a teamwork standpoint. You bring certain gifts and talents to the table and so does your partner. But you need to discuss what they are and how they will come together to make your house a happy home. Don't assume that because your mom cooked, cleaned, wash clothes, mopped the floor, helped the kids with homework, and knitted caps for everybody that your wife will do that. Maybe her cooking skills leaves a lot to the imagination. Maybe that is your area of gifting and you bring that to the table. Maybe the wife is excellent with tools and can fix anything around the house.

Sometimes we are stuck on traditional male and female roles that we force things upon people that they can't effectively handle and we get irritated because it didn't turn out to our satisfaction. Likewise, if we are not gifted in an area, it will show. Counseling is a great time to discuss in what lanes you will operate. This blueprint, which can change as you grow, will help you avoid unnecessary arguments and strife.

Planning/Problem-Solving

Planning is important for building. If you remain in the mindset of building, you will always pay close attention to what needs to be done for the team. Someone has to take the lead to make sure there is a game plan. Who is that person and what is that process? Discuss it. Do you come together and plan together? Do you have a suggestion jar in which your conversations arise? Do you come up with complete ideas and present them to your spouse? Or do you just wait for your spouse to come up with everything and you simply follow along?

Some things are based on the individuals in the relationship and their personalities. One might be an amazing planner and the other might be the executioner (no pun intended). Together, it can be a winning combination. But if you have two Type A personalities, there must be considerable give and take for anything to work successfully. You must have a process to make that happen. It starts by talking through it and understanding what you are facing. Ultimately, someone will have to make a decision. So you work together and become comfortable with allowing your spouse to make the decision or doing it together.

The same applies to problem solving. If there is a problem, it has to be solved. Who's going to handle that and how is it going to be handled? Based on your roles and responsibilities that you already identified, some of these things will work themselves out. The car breaks down and the husband is a mechanic, he'll step in and get it taken care of. The wife handles the finances? There is an irregularity in the checking account so she goes in and checks the records to find out what happened.

Counseling should help drive home the point that planning and problem solving should be discussed on a regular basis. There should not be a bunch of assumptions;

each person should know their roles and responsibilities and there should be a level of comfort in knowing who will handle what.

Maintaining Your Identity

One of the most difficult things for people to do after marriage is maintaining their individual identities. Like everything else that has been discussed, it's an ongoing process but your counselor should help identify some ways to help do that.

By having those discussions during premarital counseling, your partner will learn some areas, some people, and some activities that are important to you. It will allow them to appreciate your time in those areas and also know more about what makes you happy. You want to bring 100 percent to the relationship and that includes things that make you uniquely you. That applies to your partner as well.

Post-Marital Counseling

Tarai and I have gone to counseling a few times after premarital counseling. Sometimes our hearts were hardened and other times we were open to learning from the counselor and moving past our individual and joint issues. Every time, I got something from it. I recommend some form of counseling remain a part of a couple's on-going plan to grow. Again, growing things live and living things grow. I must drive that point home. You don't want your marriage to find a way into a stagnant black hole that opens up the door for doubt, insecurities, infidelity, boredom, or anything else that can hinder the relationship.

There was also a time when Tarai and I disagreed on whether we needed counseling. I've also counseled many couples who were at the same stage in their relationship where there was a blockage in communication, love making, and/or team building that stunted the growth of the marriage. But one or the other stated that they didn't think they needed counseling. My position has always been if one partner says there's a problem and the other says there's no problem, you *both* have a problem. So if your spouse suggests counseling, go. Maybe there are some thing that your spouse need to address in him/herself but need you there. Maybe he/she can't properly communicate issues in the marriage that a therapist might be able to assist with. Maybe there is something the spouse needs from you that can only be extracted in a controlled environment with a trained counselor. If your desire is to continue to grow and build, I recommend continued counseling after marriage, especially if one or both of you need it.

Counseling help:

- You can consider traditional wedding counseling from your church or religious leaders or from a secular private therapist. These sessions can be issue specific or they can be general. For example, if communication is becoming a stumbling block in your marriage, a counselor can help you identify areas of weakness and try to help strengthen them. But you might want a counselor just to be able to identify on-going exercises in which you can address topics as a way of avoiding potential problems. For example, one of our counselors gave us a section of a book to read and we returned with our individual perspective on the topic and discussed various views. It allowed us to read some real life scenarios and discuss how we would handle them.

- You can also participate in couples retreats and workshops which deal with specific relationships issues and exercises. Many churches have couples ministries where they have guest speakers discussing topics that most couples deal with. Sometimes you learn that what you go through is common and other couples have overcome issues. At the same time, you might hear some things that will let you know that as bad as you think your spouse is, it could be worse. Weekend couples retreats and workshops can be awesome for a few reasons – you get to fellowship with other couples; you get to work on some of the issues that face most couples; and you get to spend time alone as a couple in the midst of building your relationship in a positive, safe environment.

- There are also online seminars, workbooks, DVDs, and more than can serve as on-going marital development. Never assume that things are fine and that you have it all figured out. Always have a mindset to build and grow. That takes being proactive.

CHAPTER 9
DEALING WITH DIFFICULT TIMES

Beautiful,

I am so glad that when you wanted to walk away, you stayed and when I wanted to walk away, I stayed. We may not be where we want to be but we are together and as long as we're together, we can make anything happen. The reason that we didn't walk away and be on our own is because we were meant to fly together. So let's continue to strengthen our wings, set our destinations and soar. There is no place I'd rather be, no person I'd rather be with, or nothing I'd rather do than LIVE and BE with you! I love you a new love today and I can't wait to love you a newer love tomorrow!

Papi

I wrote Tarai that letter upon reflecting on some of the most difficult times in our marriage, that included infidelity, lack of support, and lack of desire to build and grow together. But that time of reflection also included the promises of God, the memory of the vows we shared, and the bright outlook for our future together.

Our close family members and friends know of many of the challenges we faced even before marriage and certainly after getting married. Many of them know the times when Tarai was done with me and our marriage was all but done. Many know of the times I was done with Tarai and our marriage was all but done. We were even separated for a time, living in different houses. We were also separated at other times living under the same roof. Basically, we were roommates.

For the majority of our marriage, we were seen as a model couple, perfect to many, and we did a great job of masking the true issues underneath the surface. But they couldn't be hidden long and when some of the issues rose to the surface, we had to re-evaluate who we were as individuals, who we were as a couple, and what we wanted moving forward. It wasn't an easy process. When you have lived for so long convincing others to believe a story, you start believing some things, too. You must strip back down to the foundation and rebuild. That takes a commitment from both parties and at certain times, neither Tarai nor myself were willing to do that. So that prolonged the difficult times in our marriage.

Let me give you an example of what I mean. Tarai had warned me about the time I spent with a woman, saying that nothing good would come from it. I chalked it up to her being insecure, accusatory, overreacting, and her trying to control me. Unfortunately, I didn't listen. She was right. I found myself in a horrible situation that ultimately impacted Tarai and my entire family. My selfishness jeopardized – no ruined – everything that we had built (even though some things were built on a weak foundation).

But here's what that situation revealed:

- We had more problems than we admitted.
- We had cracks in our foundation that needed to be repaired.
- We had to come from behind the masks.
- We had to make a decision if we were going to rebuild and rebuild stronger.
- We discovered who was for us and who was against us.
- And a number of individual things we needed to face.

Because she was right about that situation, to some it justified every other time she was insecure, accusatory, overreacting, and controlling. And that just wasn't so. It didn't make the situation any better. But at some point, we had to answer the question… Are we going to move forward or go our separate ways? It was one of the most difficult times of our lives. But it was something that had to be dealt with.

When we decided that we would stay together and make it work, it wasn't popular among everyone in our circles. People were in our ears telling us this is a perfect opportunity to severe ties. I've said many times, that Tarai would have been justified in walking away from the marriage and there wouldn't have been much I could say or do. But she chose to stay and make it work. And I thank God for that.

There are other examples that I can share where we were at that crossroads and we both decided we are better together than apart. But I just wanted to give you one of my transparent and vulnerable moments in our process so that you will see that dealing with difficulties in your marriage takes work.

Whether your marriage difficulties stem from infidelity, trust issues, finances, romance, broken vision, no vision, lack of support, religious views, childrearing philosophies, blended family drama, baby mama drama, or anything else, you must decide if and how you are going to move forward. Here are a few things to do at the crossroads:

- **Stop and conduct a self-assessment:** Oftentimes when we arrive at a crossroads, there is something within us that is off. Maybe we are no longer happy about a situation. Maybe we have grown and we don't feel our spouses have grown with us. Maybe there is something you need that you are not getting. Maybe you can't live up to the expectations of your spouse. Maybe the feelings of inadequacies have overtaken you and you don't know if you can make the appropriate adjustments. Maybe you have been living a lie and you just can't live with yourself that way any longer.

- **Assess the relationship:** In the process of self-assessment and self-evaluation, you'll come across several layers that will include the relationship. As mentioned above, can you fulfill your roles and responsibilities that you and your spouse discussed? If you haven't discussed those thing, can you have those discussions and agree to move forward with them as a team? What are the great things about the marriage and how can you continue them? What are the weaknesses and how can you improve them?

- **Determine what you are willing to do to improve the situation:** Sometimes, a change in you is all that's necessary if you are the reason for the problems. So own your shortcomings and be willing to make amends. Apologize if you have wronged your spouse and then work toward improving yourself, the situation and the marriage. But you must know what you are willing to do and what you are not. Those things need to be made clear to your spouse in case that is insufficient to them. But you must be on the same page, even though it begins with your willingness to deal with the situation.

- **Determine your spouse's commitment to improve the situation:** When you decide together to move forward, it's imperative that you know the same levels of commitment for each other. Because you are different and impacted differently by the situation, you won't have the same mindset but you must agree upon what you are willing to do and what you are not… for the sanity and wellbeing of each of you.

- **You must forgive:** I've heard people say, "I will forgive but I won't forget." I understand the emotion behind the pain when someone is lied to, betrayed, abused, controlled, etc. I know that doesn't just go away. But in order to move forward, you can't hold something over someone's head if you truly forgive them. Forgiveness is a challenge but building and growing are challenges as well. You can't successfully build on a foundation or pillars of unforgiveness. That could be an individual issue that one spouse has to work on.

- **Develop a plan to move forward:** It's one thing to decide you're going to stay and make your marriage work but it means nothing without a strategy to succeed. I am a big proponent of progress. I preach it, teach it, practice it, and share it. Devise a manageable plan that includes achievable goals that assist rebuilding the marriage. For example, if finances are what's causing the blockage, create weekly or monthly accounting or budgeting sessions so you can improve the financial situation in the marriage. Or maybe you can find a counselor to help with whatever the issue is. If you don't already have a marriage mission statement, develop one. This can be your constant reminder of why you are together. It can be simple or more detailed to include a family crest and pillars. Display them prominently so you can always refer to them.

- **Be willing to sacrifice:** If you are in a difficult situation in your marriage, whether you are the cause or not, you must be willing to sacrifice for the common good of the union. Oftentimes, it's hard for the hurt person to accept that they, too, must sacrifice but it has to be a team effort even in the rebuilding stage. At the same time, be honest with yourself. Know what you are willing to give up and what you are willing to do to make the marriage work. At the same time, set your standard for what you are not willing to sacrifice or do. That could determine how, or if, the rebuild happens.

- **Find ways to celebrate:** Celebrate the small victories and the large victories along the way. Some people work so hard on fixing things, they forget the reason they are fixing it. You must enjoy each other in the process. If you don't, the process itself will exhaust you and have you resenting your spouse. In your plan, include celebrations, dates nights, and opportunities to reminisce on the good times. It goes a long way in building momentum while creating new memories.

- **God is our foundation:** With all that Tarai and I have been through in the 30 years that we've known each other and the 23 years that we've been married, people often ask me what's the secret. I simply tell them, "When she wanted to leave, she didn't. When I wanted to leave, I didn't." The reasons may vary at different times and I don't want to speak for Tarai. But I have often said, how can I say that I believe Tarai is the woman that God created for me and give up when things get difficult. Unless I no longer believe in God or for some reason God doesn't want

Tari for me or me for Tarai, I'm going to do whatever it takes to make sure we continue to live and grow together. So sometimes it takes returning to that foundation… God, the Bible, his vision for my life, his vision for her life, and his vision for our lives together. Even when that's a challenge, we must decide to work through it together. I admonish you to do the same.

CHAPTER 10
A PERFECT MOMENT

There are not many things I enjoy more than seeing my wife smile. One of them is being the reason she smiles. Overall, I'm a laidback kind of guy with no need for over-the-top antics, theatrics, or drama (unless I'm writing them, of course). But when it comes to putting that smile on her face and enjoying the moment, there's no telling what I would do. Out of the blue, I might walk into the room 'bucket naked', swinging in the wind, doing a silly dance, just for the moment of putting that smile on her face and cherishing the seconds or minutes she laughs. Or, we might be taking an 'usie' and I'll make a goofy face without her knowing. Then when she sees the picture, she can't help but laugh. Those are the moments and memories that you cherish for a lifetime. It's indeed priceless. No amount of money, no material item, or promises of fame and fortune can compare.

Several years back, I wrote her a simple poem to explain what I mean. It's called A Perfect Moment. The original poem is somewhere buried in a storage bin. But the essence of the poem says that a perfect moment is when it's just the two of us, time stands still, and nothing else matters. During that time, we don't think about the bills that are due; issues with family or friends; work; church; or anything else that might surface outside of that perfect moment. We just engulf ourselves in each other in that moment and enjoy it to the fullest.

Most of the time, perfect moments just happen. You both notice something funny, look at each other and bust out laughing. A song comes on and you jump up and dance together. You're driving home from a long day, spot rainbow and decide to step out the car to take a picture. Back in the car, you have a heart-felt conversation about the promises of

God. Those are perfect moments that happen.

But recently, I've come to the conclusion that sometimes you have to make an extra effort to create perfect moments. Remember, it's not about how big or small the gesture is; the moment is what makes it perfect. For example, you know the things that arouse a response in your mate. Maybe they love when you wear a certain outfit that you hate. Wear it! Maybe they like unexpected visits to their job bearing flowers. Maybe it's a surprise trip because your spouse has been stressed at work.

Tarai heard me mention that I was looking at a waffle maker online. Not long after, she gave me a waffle maker as a gift. On our 22nd anniversary, we took a helicopter ride. She smiled the whole time, asking how I knew that's what she was considering. And, we both had custom t-shirts designed celebrating the anniversary since 22 has been a significant number for us since moving to Georgia. Those were perfect moments that we created because we understand the significance of perfect moments.

I'm not one to experiment when it comes to food. I like what I like and that's what I eat. Tarai often tells me to broaden my palate. But I brush it off because I'm good with my pizza and meat and potatoes. So she can keep her teriyaki chicken, her Mexican corn, and her black beans, cabbage and rice! She's learned over the years not even to ask me if I want some. Well, actually she still tries but out of habit. Anyway, every now and again, I'll ask her for a taste. After going back and forth about whether I'm going to waste her food, I will try something. Her reaction to my reaction is priceless. We already knew that it would disgust me, but that little gesture could create a perfect moment that we can look back on and smile. "Remember, when you tried my Cajun shrimp and made that stink face?"

There was another time when I stopped by the store on the way home and grabbed a couple movies on DVD and two bags full of junk food – potato chips, Swedish fish, lemon heads, popcorn, candy bars, etc. Every now and then, we just chill at home and binge on unhealthy snacks. We sat up in the bed with all our snacks, our movies and each other. It was a perfect moment that was even better than I could have imagined. We'll still say, "Remember our junk food date?"

There are other examples that start off the same way, "Remember…"

The problem with trying to manufacture perfect moments is you run the risk of the attempt falling short. It happens. Know that sometimes your jokes will fall flat. Something you do will inevitably cause anger rather than joy. And… you just might get flat out rejected. But here's the thing, I look at it like I did with sales; it's a numbers game. The more you try, the better your chances of experiencing that once in a lifetime moment over and over again. It's like a perfect moment déjà vu.

When things aren't going well and you find yourself in the doghouse or if you are faced with the possibility of calling it quits, look back on those perfect moments. Think about the times when you looked into each other's eyes and you knew you never experienced anything like that before. Remember that feeling when you felt yourself falling in love like it was the first time. Ask yourself this… Will I be okay without ever experiencing that again? Nine times out of 10, the answer is no. A perfect moment defines that particular space in time but it also lays the foundation for future perfect moments.

Before my mother in-law died, my father in-law and I sat on the porch talking about all the issues he had over the years with his wife and all the issues I had over the years with his daughter. Our venting quickly turned to the perfect moments in our marriages. We both agreed that having to endure the challenging times paid off during those perfect moments.

Cherish your perfect moments and find ways to create more.

C. NATHANIEL BROWN

ABOUT THE AUTHOR

C. Nathaniel Brown is an award-winning writer, publisher, speaker, and filmmaker. He is author of several bestselling books, including *Shift Happens Then You Live*; *Xs, Os, and Ws: Inspirational Stories from Successful Basketball Coaches*; *Devil in the Mirror: Overcoming the Enemy's Attack*; and *The Business of My Book*, a guide to help writers understand the business side of writing. The Baltimore native is a sought-after speaker on topics such as Telling Your Story, Men's Issues, Empowerment, Discovering Your Passion and Purpose, and more. As a writing coach, he assists writers develop concepts, overcome writers block and navigate through the publishing process. As an award-winning filmmaker, Brown has written, produced and directed nearly two dozen films, including *Chi Nu Legacy*, a feature film that addresses campus sexual assault; *Same Spot*; *55 Seconds*; and *The Interview*. Brown resides in Atlanta, Ga., with his wife Tarai.

Stay Connected with C. Nathaniel Brown:
www.CNathanielBrown.com
Facebook: www.Facebook.com/CNathanielBrown11
Twitter: @CNathanielBrown
Instagram: @CNathanielBrown
Google+: @CNathanielBrown
Youtube: @CNathanielBrown

Feel free to share your reviews of
Baking Pies & Making Love
at email ExpectedEndEntertainment@gmail.com,
or on Amazon.com.

OTHER TITLES BY C. NATHANIEL BROWN

- I Love You: 365 Reasons and Love Letters
- Shift Happens Then You Live: Take Control of Your Life and Win
- Shift Happens Then You Live: The 30-Day Prayer Companion
- Reflections on Purpose
- Dear Depression
- I Always Put the Seat Down
- Devil in the Mirror: Overcoming the Enemy's Attack
- Xs, Os, and Ws: Inspirational Stories from Successful Basketball Coaches
- The Hair Commandments: Shalls and Shall Nots of Wigs, Weaves, and Natural Hair
- The Business of My Book: Make More Money, Reach More People by Understanding the Business of Being a Writer
- Making Wings: Short Stories and Poems
- Take Your Message to the Masses: 8 Reasons Why Every Minister Should Publish a Book

For more information or to order these titles, visit
www.cnathanielbrown.com

www.ingramcontent.com/pod-product-compliance
Lightning Source LLC
Chambersburg PA
CBHW071229090426
42736CB00014B/3015